Why the Confederacy Lost

Why the Confederacy Lost

Edited by
GABOR S. BORITT

Essays by

JAMES M. MCPHERSON
ARCHER JONES
GARY W. GALLAGHER
REID MITCHELL
JOSEPH T. GLATTHAAR

New York Oxford Oxford University Press

Oxford University Press

Oxford New York Toronto
Delhi Bombay Calcutta Madras Karachi
Kuala Lumpur Singapore Hong Kong Tokyo
Nairobi Dar es Salaam Cape Town
Melbourne Auckland Madrid

and associated companies in
Berlin Ibadan

First published in 1992 by Oxford University Press, Inc.,
200 Madison Avenue, New York, New York 10016

First issued as an Oxford University Press paperback, 1993

Oxford is a registered trademark of Oxford University Press

Library of Congress Cataloging-in-Publication Data
Why the Confederacy lost / edited by Gabor S. Boritt ;
essays by James M. McPherson . . . [et al.].
p. cm. Includes bibliographical references and index.
ISBN 0-19-507405-X
ISBN 0-19-508549-3 (pbk.)
1. United States—History—Civil War, 1861–1865.
2. Confederate States of America—History.
I. Boritt, G. S., 1940– .
II. McPherson, James M.
E464.W48 1992 973.7—dc20 91-44291

10 9 8 7 6 5 4 3 2

Printed in the United States of America

for
Anjörn Nockesson
and his descendants
in the 19th and 20th generations
at Gettysburg
They teach me about life
ב ה

Acknowledgments

By late June it is usually warm, even hot in Gettysburg. In the night at our farm the fire flies glow in the dark, fleeting specks illuminating the woods and turning Marsh Creek into a pageant. In the daytime along the side of the road orange tiger lilies proclaim their eternal message. My heart overflows; it is time to see old friends again, time to make new ones, it is the time of the Gettysburg Civil War Institute.

This book is the product of that Institute, 1991. We meet each year during the week before the anniversary of the Battle. Our goal is to bring to the literate general public history that many will find irresistible and do this without abandoning solid scholarly moorings. Students range from sixteen to the eighties. A high school junior, on a scholarship provided by CWI alumni, may find a United States Ambassador on one side of her, and the athletic director of Pennsylvania State University on the other.

Our speakers are some of the finest historians of the Civil War. They come to discuss their past contributions to scholarship, their work in progress, or, as is the case this year, consider a topic assigned to them. For example in 1986 Robert V. Bruce addressed the impact of war on science and technology—a lecture that was tied to a tour of Harpers Ferry. In 1987 he returned as a student. In 1988, his *The Launching of Modern American Science, 1846–1876* (1987) won the Pulitzer Prize in history. He continued to return as a student, but was promoted to "scholar in residence." To provide another illustration: James McPherson repeatedly tried out his ideas for *The Battle Cry of Freedom* (1988) at Gettysburg. That work also received the Pulitzer. And so it goes.

Battlefield tours are part of the program, too, and each year the CWI visits a different place and tours Gettysburg as well. The contrast between the beautiful, peaceful fields and the grim memories they hold, provides instruction that is hard to match in the classroom.

And so each year at Gettysburg, we all understand, mythology and history meet, struggling to come to terms with each other. But for the historian, mythology (or the more simple nostalgia) is both a friend and an enemy. He must replace illusion with reality as he can best find it, but replace it so as not to demolish the love for history.

In 1991, as we turned to the question Why the Confederacy Lost, many fine people helped make the Gettysburg CWI and, soon after, this book, a reality. Tina Fair ran, and runs, my office with energy, competence, flair, and a firm hand. She is assisted by two blithe and efficient spirits, Charlene Locke and Linda Marshall. Among them they performed numerous chores, managed to get the chapters of this book in the computer, make successive revisions, and somehow, along the way, did not complain. Robert M. Sandow, Gettysburg College, Class of '92, my research assistant, carefully checked the quotations in this book against the original sources, saving his elders but in this case not betters, from many a small embarrassment. Sheldon Meyer of Oxford University Press was encouraging and efficient in his work with me, as was Leona Capeless, my editor. Peter Sandler created the index for the book.

At the 1991 CWI we all felt fortunate to be assisted by Dr. William F. Hanna and a group of bright students: Ellen Abrahamson, Jonathan Berkey, Christina Ericson, Jennifer Haase, Richard Hoffman, Jennifer Horner, Craig Montesano, and two of my sons: Jake and Dan Boritt.

As the last two names indicate, my work, and this book, are a family affair. Liz my wife helped—always. Norse created the design for the dedication page, inspired by traditional Pennsylvania Dutch motifs and the lettering of the *Beowulf* manuscript at the British Library. Jake, full of fun and good ideas, worked full-time at the CWI; Daniel, a bright, hard worker at ten, "only" part-time. To them go my deep thanks and to the children also a bit of Lincoln apocrypha: "I don't know who my grandfather was but I'm much more interested in what his grandson will do." If this is a bit anti-historical, it is also very American.

The contributors to this book deserve special acknowledgment. Our time together at the Gettysburg CWI was a pleasure. We have kept in touch since. They delivered their papers by the deadlines, made prompt revisions, helped each other generously, and showed much goodwill. Robert Bruce joined our one seminar discussion and added his wit and good sense. I am grateful for such colleagues.

I am thankful also for the happy, loyal, and intelligent students of history who come to the Gettysburg CWI. May there be many like them in every corner of the country, and the globe.

The final word of thanks goes to Gettysburg College for understanding that history is important.

The book is dedicated to a dim memory from early Scandinavian history and to some very real, dear people in Gettysburg at the end of the second millennium. Had I placed professional obligations above such people, the book would be dedicated to David Donald, Richard Current, and Norman Graebner, and to the memory of David Potter and T. Harry Williams.

Summer 1991 Gabor Boritt
Farm by the Ford
Gettysburg

Contents

Introduction

GABOR S. BORITT

JOSHUA CHAMBERLAIN'S VOICE rang clear: "Bayonet!" The command "ran like fire along the line, from man to man, and rose into a shout." Abandoning their protected positions up on the hill, the Twentieth Maine "sprang forward" and charged *down* "upon the enemy."[1]

Gettysburg, July 2, 1863. Little Round Top. The very end of the Union flank. Defend the ground at all cost. Men from Alabama attack. Up the slope into the Union line they tear, and as they retreat leave their dead behind, and those of Maine. Then up they charge again, and again. The New England line almost doubles back upon itself, forming a narrow "V," trying to defend its flank, and rear too. Nearly two hours go by. Up on the hill ammunition runs low. Yet the Rebels seem ready to charge again. As dusk comes, bodies, cries, smoke, and dread cover the rocky hillside. Chamberlain cannot hold on. He must do something. He is in command. "Bayonet!" Countercharge down the slope. The "V" rights itself into a straight line as the surprise plunge down the hill starts. Then a great wheeling movement. A company at one end serves as the pivot and the blue-coated line sweeps all before it. To a Pennsylvania officer observing the sight, the soldiers from Maine—fishermen, lumbermen, farmers—seemed to move "like a great gate upon a post."[2]

When that gate shut, so did perhaps the best hope of the Confederacy shut down at Gettysburg. Little Round Top was "the key" to the whole Union position.[3] Had it fallen the road would have opened to the Yankee rear for the Army of Northern Virginia. The Federal line on Cemetery Ridge would have become untenable, especially with Confederate artillery above it. General Robert E. Lee would have had another victory, this time on northern soil. Could that have been the decisive battle so many looked for? Years later Colonel William C. Oates, the commander of the men from Alabama, paid homage to his counterpart, the college professor turned colonel from Maine, who with "his men saved Little Round Top and the Army of the Potomac from defeat." Oates added: "Great events sometimes turn on comparatively small affairs."[4]

Of course this little sketch suggests too much. Certainly for Chamberlain, who by now has entered Civil War mythology. It is true that his Twentieth Maine defended exceptionally well the potential anchor of the Union left flank. But other units, too, played important roles in saving Little Round Top. The significance of the Battle of Gettysburg for the war as a whole can be questioned, too. After all, the bibliography for that battle alone is a 277-page book that now needs to be supplemented.[5] As for the possibility of Confederate victory—what might have been we can never be sure of.

Yet looking at history in terms of "the might have beens" is not only defensible but at times so illuminating as to be indispensable. The French thinker Raymond Aron lamented years ago how "always and everywhere . . .

> there are discovered underlying and *valid* reasons which retrospectively confer an apparent necessity upon the effective outcome. It is forgotten that the opposite outcome might perhaps have permitted an equally satisfactory explanation. . . . Retrospection creates an *illusion of fatality* which contradicts the contemporary *impression of contingency*. Neither one is *a priori* true or false. . . .[6]

In short, overlooking "the might have beens" may prevent the full understanding of "the have beens" that make up history.

Chamberlain's story at Gettysburg also points toward an axiom undergirding this book. Matters military, including what took place on the field of battle, played a decisive role in determining the history of the Civil War, and specifically why the Confederacy lost. This statement is so self-evident as to make one who utters it look simpleminded. Yet many professional historians do not seem to grasp this simple truth.

To illustrate, a professor at one of the principal southern universities created an anthology of readings about the Civil War era that ignored totally the military side of the war. The book must have been a popular assignment on campuses because it came out in a second edition, too.[7] In a like spirit, a distinguished historian from a major northern university edited for the American Historical Association (the largest body of historians in the United States), a volume intended to bring the wisdom and learning of the university to high school teachers. The essay covering the Civil War observed at the outset that "No period of our nation's history has proved as perennially fascinating to Americans." It then proceeded to ignore entirely the *war*—at least as that word is commonly understood. In addition to its deep prejudice about the nature of history, the work shows an equally deep misunderstanding of contemporary American popular culture.[8]

And the Organization of American Historians (the other chief scholarly body, for specialists on the past of the United States alone) provides a Civil War prize. However, it proscribes books with primarily military orientations. Though such books are sometimes mindless, it is reasonably clear that their complete exclusion reflects not merely the will and Quaker faith of the award's donor but also the biases of many historians and of intellectuals in general.[9]

It might be noted that on the most recent occasion when the OAH prize was presented to a winner, the reading of the terms of the award was greeted by laughter from the audience. Hope then remains that common sense shall yet prevail. Calling for a fuller understanding of the war by professional historians is not to decry the impulse to focus on meaning, on causes and results rather than means. Nor must it be forgotten that the current generation has produced some remarkably fine works on the Civil War era—both in the military area and, much more, outside of it. History has many faces and even in a war the battlefield and related matters constitute only one. But ignoring that face and its meaning—however distasteful to many, however ugly war is—distorts the past grievously.

Why the Confederacy Lost has a dominant military coloration. We agree with Lincoln's judgment, rendered in his second inaugural address in 1865, that upon "the progress of our arms . . . all else chiefly" depended.[10] I began to outline this book while America was at war, early in 1991. All but one of the contributors started work on their essays as the war progressed and all completed their work in its immediate aftermath. We all know that contemporary events cannot but influence historical interpretation. I wondered then, and do now, how the war with Iraq has influenced this book. Surely, as a minimum, it reinforced our belief that, for good or for ill, war leaves deep marks.

I encouraged each contributor to make his own strong case. I promised to explain in the Introduction that, for example, though one of us will emphasize the role of the common soldiers to Union victory, this does not mean that he fails to understand that generals had something to do with the outcome, too. And so it goes.

Since 1865 much thought has gone into the question why the Confederacy lost the war. James McPherson begins this book by noting the importance of the question: "Rare is the Civil War historian who does not have something to say on this subject, at least implicitly."

Surveying the answers given, from participants like Robert E. Lee and George Pickett to historians in our own time, McPherson divides proposed explanations into two categories: (1) *internal,* focused primarily on what took place within the Confederacy; (2) *external,* with emphasis on elements that accounted for northern victory. Both categories of explanation seem to assume Confederate defeat to be inevitable. McPherson reviews these interpretations, which cover the range from slavery, politics, economics, morale, and leadership to class conflict—and he rejects them all. In their place he proposes the theory of contingency: either side might have won. For, ultimately, the battlefield gave birth to victory. He thus focuses on military history, albeit not the spread-eagle blow-the-bugle variety. Perhaps the greatest pleasure of the essay is its good common sense combined with the insight it provides into historical reasoning.

If the outcome of the war was determined on the battlefield the question of the means used there becomes potentially important. Yet Archer Jones's examination of both Confederate and Union strategies concludes that neither got the better of the other. Though the political and military leaders rarely came forth with explicit statements on the subject, Jones reconstructs their strategies with a sure hand. He distinguishes between raiding and persisting advance as well as between logistic and combat strategy. He shows how both sides relied on Napoleonic ways with turning movements and concentration of forces. The Rebels also used successful cavalry and guerrilla raids. Late in the war Grant, too, adopted raiding with devastating force. Throughout, Jones never loses sight of the intimate connection of strategy to politics. In the end the two sides balanced each other. And so the imaginative student is left with questions: Could the Union have improved its strategy and so shortened the war? Conversely: Could the Confederates have improved their strategy and so tipped the balance to victory?

Gary Gallagher's look at the role of generals in Confederate defeat suggests the answer to the last question: Lee, the architect of Rebel strategy, pursued the best available course. If Jones's essay found, surprisingly, that excellent strategy on both sides canceled each other out, leading towards a draw, and therefore made no difference in the outcome of the war, Gallagher maintains that "it is impossible to discuss the reasons for northern victory or southern defeat without coming to terms" with the dominant part played by generals. Comparisons of these officers with each other, McPherson warned, amounts to "a minefield through which historians had better maneuver carefully." However, Gallagher wades in—with care but also in a provocative way.

He takes a hard look at the leading officers, Yankee and Rebel, and eliminates all but three whose decisions substantially shaped the war: Grant, Sherman, and Lee. No other generals influenced military matters in comparable ways though there were many others with much talent. Grant deserves the lion's share of credit for the Union triumph. Together with Sherman he provided the strategy and the victories that, in time, won the war.

These conclusions appear to be no longer controversial, but Lee's part in the war continues to be debated heatedly. Perhaps because the Virginian has been treated for so long as a demigod, the mythological counterpart of Lincoln (rather than Grant, his most likely historical counterpart), a new generation of scholars raised sharp questions about the southern master of battlefields. Some doubt his ability to see the large picture, that beyond Richmond and Virginia, and suggest that his aggressive style of fighting shortened the life of the Confederacy. Gallagher presents fairly the case against Lee and offers his own solid defense. Displaying a clear understanding of the dependence of diplomacy, politics, and the morale of society as a whole on the battlefield, the essay argues that the war could be won only in the East and that only Lee had a chance to win it. A good part of the credit for his not doing so must go to Grant and Sherman.

If generals made a large difference in the war, Reid Mitchell proposes that the common soldiers made an even larger one. The preponderance of resources, including manpower, favored the Union, and "as usual, God was on the side of the heaviest battalions"—or so Richard N. Current replied to the question why the North won.[11] The question for Mitchell, however, is, How did the Union succeed in employing the heaviest battalions? And conversely, How did the Confederacy in the end fail to keep even their weaker battalions in the field? Vietnam taught a generation that resources alone do not guarantee victory.

To win, armies had to be deeply motivated. In the 1860s national ideologies and small-unit cohesion created the inspiration that held the armies together. For the northern fighting man love for both the Union and his military family provided the strength to endure to the end. For the Confederate soldier small-unit cohesion played a similar role, and love of the Southern nation took the place of Union. These loyalties, however, were not equally strong on the two sides and changed over time.

Mitchell thus combines traditional military history with the "new" social history. He applies the metaphor of family to both the small army unit and the nation; he sees them, respectively, "a man's family writ large" and very large. But the family the soldier left behind at home also performed a crucial role in the outcome of the war. By late 1864, while the Yankee soldier stayed in the field and in the trench, the Confederate fighting man voted for his family with his feet and went home, deserting in substantial numbers. He abandoned with regret his unit and his nation. Developments on the battlefield as well as at home account for why the family, as we traditionally understand the term, prevailed over duty to fellow soldiers and country. Lee merely recognized the facts when in the spring of 1865 he conceded that the Confederacy had become "morally and physically unable to maintain the contest." The common soldiers' commitments had led both armies to Appomattox.

Mitchell remarks that the part played by black soldiers in the Union army is "just entering the realm of national myth." And high time it is as Joseph Glatthaar's essay makes clear, though he tries to avoid racial cheerleading. For long the general public seemed to be aware principally of the slaves' contribution to the Confederate cause and saw them as passive recipients of emancipation. Indeed the captive laborer, for whom revolt would have been suicidal, made it possible for southern whites to throng to the Rebel flag in large numbers. In Louisiana, for example, African-American militia even volunteered to fight under that flag and for their homes—only to be turned down. As the war went on, however, and circumstances changed, the same men fought for the Union—even as the black peoples of the nation, as a whole, came to play an increasingly important role in Confederate defeat. In the process they helped redefine the meaning of freedom in America.

The black role in the Civil War deserves special attention for solid historical reasons, which include ethical judgments. Though many other ethnic groups contributed to Union victory, none was central to the cataclysm of the mid-nineteenth century. "Blacks were at the very heart of the Civil

War," Glatthaar writes. In the South as the war progressed they increasingly deserted to the "enemy," sabotaged the slave system, and made whites who stayed at home feel often uncomfortable or threatened. In the same time the Lincoln administration moved slowly but steadily to employ blacks as laborers on military projects, then, with the pivot of emancipation, as soldiers on garrison and transportation duties, and finally as combat troops. Nearly 190,000 served in the Union army and navy and so in the fight for their own freedom. The stories of the men of the Civil War are the stuff of legend. But none suffered as much, none had as great obstacles to overcome as blacks did, to reach, for example, the parapet of Fort Wagner, and glory.

Glatthaar argues that "the timely and extensive" African-American military participation "made the difference between a Union victory and stalemate or defeat." The historian goes almost as far as Lincoln did in 1864 when he wrote bluntly, and as it turned out for his own eyes only, about the force of the black soldiers. "Keep it and you can save the Union. Throw it away, and the Union goes with it." With such words the president defended from political opponents his joint policy of emancipation and putting black men into the army. But a year earlier he went to his countrymen with equally blunt words looking ahead to victory:

> And then, there will be some black men who can remember that, with silent tongue, and clenched teeth, and steady eye, and well-poised bayonet, they have helped mankind on to this great consummation; while, I fear, there will be some white ones, unable to forget that, with malignant heart, and deceitful speech, they have strove to hinder it.[12]

We chose the title of the book deliberately (even though it makes this volume an exception to the categorization provided in James McPherson's essay). Use of the word "South" in place of the "Confederacy" is a misnomer, however much sanctioned by tradition. A significant part of the South was black and by the end of the war nearly all of it anti-Confederate in feeling. A percentage of the white South was Unionist as well. Close to half of the South probably welcomed northern victory. Of course the North, too, was divided, but no appreciable segment hoped for Confederate triumph. Thus using the term "North" for the one side is much more reasonable than using "South" for the other.

One might even argue that over the long run the South (and with it the United States and the world) was better off with Confederate defeat. For this reason, too, we should not search for the explanations of the outcome of the war under the title "Why the South Lost": it did not. The Confederacy did—a particular and very important outgrowth of the South. All the same the reader will find us inevitably backsliding, to improve our style (the word "Confederate" can be repeated only so often), in the spirit of compromise, and to make use of the pungent quotation.

This book follows in the footsteps of a similar volume published in 1960 under the editorship of David Donald, *Why the North Won the Civil War.* That book and this are based on conferences held at Gettysburg College, in 1958 and 1991, respectively. The earlier historians looked at various facets of the war such as economics, politics, and so on. We focus on military matters and thus we do not so much replace as supplement the earlier book. That it was time to take another look at the question of *Why* is clear enough. Unlike the earlier scholars, we all agree with McPherson concerning the contingent nature of history. In the Civil War either side might have won. In philosophical terms then we lean against determinism. We agree, too, that the battlefield cannot be separated from society and politics. The surprising degree of harmony these essays display, however, is not perfect. If we hope to be true to life, and to history, it cannot be.

1

American Victory, American Defeat

JAMES M. MCPHERSON

EFFORTS TO EXPLAIN the causes of Confederate defeat in the Civil War have generated a great deal of controversy over the past century and a quarter. The debate began with the publication in 1866 of *The Lost Cause* by Richmond journalist Edward Pollard, who blamed Jefferson Davis. Numerous books and articles since then have addressed the issue explicitly in their titles, as did the anthology of essays first presented as lectures at Gettysburg College in 1958, *Why the North Won the Civil War,* and the volume published in 1986 co-authored by four historians, *Why the South Lost the Civil War.* Many other books suggest by their titles an answer to the question of why the Confederacy lost, including Frank Owsley's *State Rights in the Confederacy,* Paul Escott's *After Secession: Jefferson Davis and the Failure of Southern Nationalism,* and Grady McWhiney's and Perry D. Jamieson's *Attack and Die: Civil War Military Tactics and the Southern Heritage.* Rare is the Civil War historian who does not have something to say on this subject, at least implicitly. Judging from the questions provoked by the essays in the present volume when they were delivered as lectures at Gettysburg College's annual Civil War Institute in June 1991, the subject remains as vital as ever.

Yet despite all the efforts to explain Why the North Won or Why the South Lost—the difference in phraseology is sometimes significant—we still do not have a consensus. The books and essays cited in the previous paragraph offer a variety of explanations. In fact, dozens of different interpretations have come forth during the past 125 years. This suggests that a definitive answer is not possible. That will not stop us from trying to come up with one, though—nor should it. If definitive truth were possible in history, historians would soon have nothing left to write about. The following critical review of the literature on the reasons for Confederate defeat will disclose that I do not pretend to have a definitive answer. But this review may shed new light on the question at hand as well as on other important matters central to the meaning of the Civil War.

Most interpretations fall into one of two categories: internal or external. Internal explanations focus mainly or entirely on the Confederacy, and usually phrase the question as "Why the South Lost." External interpretations look at both the Union and Confederacy, and often phrase it as "Why the North Won." No matter which approach they take, most studies assume, at least implicitly, that Union victory was inevitable. My analysis of these interpretations should make clear that I think an external approach more sensible but that I do *not* regard the outcome to have been inevitable.

To illustrate the difference between an internal and external interpretation, let us look at the battle of Gettysburg as a microcosm of the larger issue. Most of the controversy that has swirled endlessly for the past 128 years has focused on the issue of why the Confederates *lost* that battle—an *internal* explanation. Contemporaries and historians have blamed almost every prominent Confederate general at Gettysburg for mistakes that lost the battle: among them Robert E. Lee himself for mismanagement, overconfidence, and poor judgment; Jeb Stuart for riding off on a raid around the Union army and losing contact with his own army, leaving Lee blind in the enemy's country; Richard Ewell and Jubal Early for failing to attack Cemetery Hill on the afternoon of July 1st and again for tardiness in attacking on the 2nd; and above all, James Longstreet for lack of cooperation, promptness, and vigor in the assaults of July 2nd and 3rd. It was left to George Pickett to put his finger on the problem with all of these explanations. When someone asked Pickett after the war who was responsible for Confederate defeat at Gettysburg, he scratched his head, and replied: "I've always thought the Yankees had something to do with it."

Pickett's answer was an external explanation. And, in a larger sense, so has been the most durable and perhaps most popular explanation for Northern victory in the war as a whole. It was advanced by Robert E. Lee himself in his farewell address to his soldiers at Appomattox: "The Army of Northern Virginia has been compelled to yield to overwhelming numbers and resources." This interpretation enabled southerners to preserve their pride in the courage and skill of Confederate soldiers, to reconcile defeat with their sense of honor, even to maintain faith in the righteousness of their cause while admitting that it had been lost. The Confederacy, in other words, lost the war not because it fought badly, or because its soldiers lacked courage, or because its cause was wrong, but simply because the enemy had more men and guns. As one proud Virginian expressed it: "They never whipped us, Sir, unless they were four to one. If we had had anything like a fair chance, or less disparity of numbers, we should have won our cause and established our independence."[1]

Many Yankees echoed this overwhelming-numbers-and-resources argument. While northerners believed they had won because they fought for a better cause, many of them were also ready to agree with Napoleon's maxim that God is on the side of the biggest battalions. At that earlier Gettysburg symposium on "Why the North Won," Richard Current provided a modern version of this interpretation. After reviewing the statistics of northern population and economic preponderance—two and one-half times the South's population, three times its railroad capacity, nine times its industrial production, and so on—Current concluded that "surely, in view of the disparity of resources, it would have taken a miracle . . . to enable the South to win. As usual, God was on the side of the heaviest battalions."[2]

Most recently, Shelby Foote reiterated this thesis in his own inimitable fashion. "The North fought that war with one hand behind its back," he told Ken Burns on camera in the PBS documentary "The Civil War." If necessary, added Foote, "the North simply would have brought that other arm out from behind its back. I don't think the South ever had a chance to win that war."[3] Here was inevitability in its starkest form.

Some southerners, however, began to question this overwhelming-numbers-and-resources thesis soon after the war, and by the twentieth century most of them rejected it. For while this explanation did credit to Confederate skill and courage in holding out for so long against such great odds, it seemed to do little credit to their intelligence. After all, southerners in 1861 were well aware of their disadvantages in numbers and resources. Yet they went to war confident of victory. Were they simple-minded? Irrational? Inexcusably arrogant?

As they reflected on this matter, numerous southerners and historians came to the conclusion that overwhelming-numbers-and-resources were not the cause of northern victory after all. History offered many examples of a society winning a war against greater odds than the Confederacy faced. For Americans the outstanding example, of course, was the war of independence against mighty Britain. Other precedents also came easily to southern minds in 1861: the Netherlands against Spain in the sixteenth century; Greece against the Ottoman Empire in the 1820's. In our own post-Vietnam generation we are familiar with the truth that victory does not necessarily ride with the biggest battalions.

In the Civil War the Confederacy waged a strategically defensive war to protect its territory from conquest and preserve its armies from annihilation. To "win" that kind of war, Confederate armies did not have to invade and conquer the North; they needed only to hold out long enough to force the North to the conclusion that the price of conquering the South and annihilating its armies was too high, as Britain had concluded in 1781 and as the United States concluded with respect to Vietnam in 1972. Most southerners thought in 1861 that their resources were more than sufficient to win on these terms. Most outside observers agreed. The military analyst for the *Times* of London wrote that "no war of independence ever terminated unsuccessfully except where the disparity of force was far greater than it is in this case. . . . Just as England during the revolution had to give up conquering the colonies so the North will have to give up conquering the South."[4]

Even after losing the war, many southerners continued to insist that this reasoning remained sound. In his memoirs, General Joseph E. Johnston maintained that the southern people had not been "guilty of the high crime of undertaking a war without the means of waging it successfully." And General Pierre G. T. Beauregard made the same point in 1884: "No people ever warred for independence with more relative advantages than the Confederates."[5] To be sure, Johnston and Beauregard had an axe to grind: they blamed the inept leadership of Jefferson Davis for Confederate defeat, partly in a self-serving effort to divert blame from themselves.

We shall return to that question later; for now it can be said that the overwhelming-numbers-and-resources argument has lost considerable favor among historians. The co-authors of *Why the South Lost the Civil War* maintain that "an invader needs more force than the North possessed to conquer such a large country as the South, even one so limited in logistical resources."[6] This might go a bit too far; if read literally, it seems to say that the North could not have won the war. Perhaps a better way to state it would be: To win the kind of war that the Civil War became by 1863, the North had to conquer vast stretches of southern territory, cripple southern resources, and destroy the fighting power of Confederate armies; therefore northern superiority in manpower and resources was a *necessary* but not a *sufficient* cause of victory—that is, the North could not have won without that superiority, but it alone does not explain Union victory.

Recognizing the defects in the overwhelming-numbers-and-resources theory, a number of historians developed internal explanations for Confederate defeat. One such approach focused on what might be termed an "internal conflict" thesis: The Confederacy lost because it was plagued by dissent and divisions that undercut the strong and united effort necessary to win the war. Exponents of this interpretation have emphasized various kinds of internal conflict.

One of the earliest and most persistent themes was spelled out by Frank Owsley in his book *State Rights in the Confederacy,* published in 1925. Owsley maintained that the centrifugal force of state rights fatally handicapped the efforts of the central government and of the army to mobilize men and resources for the war. Owsley singled out Governors Joseph E. Brown of Georgia and Zebulon Vance of North Carolina as guilty of obstructive policies, of withholding men and arms from the Confederate army to build up their state militias, and of debilitating political warfare against the Jefferson Davis administration. On the tombstone of the Confederacy, wrote Owsley, should be carved the epitaph "Died of State Rights."[7]

A variant on the state rights thesis focuses on the resistance by many southerners, including some national leaders like Vice President Alexander H. Stephens, to such war measures as conscription, certain taxes, suspension of the writ of *habeas corpus,* and martial law. Opponents based their denunciations of these "despotic" measures on grounds of civil liberty, or state rights, or democratic individualism, or all three combined. This opposition crippled the army's ability to fill its ranks, obtain food and supplies, and stem desertions, according to this interpretation. It hindered the government's capacity to crack down on anti-war activists who divided the southern people and sapped their will to win. The persistence during the war of the democratic practices of individualism, dissent, and carping criticism of the government caused historian David Donald, writing in 1960, to amend that inscription on the Confederacy's tombstone to "Died of Democracy."[8]

This internal conflict thesis suffers from three flaws as an explanation for Confederate defeat. First, recent scholarship has demonstrated that the negative effects on the Confederate war effort of state-rights sentiment have been much exaggerated. State leaders like Brown and Vance did indeed feud with the Davis administration and criticize the president's leadership. But at the same time these governors, and others, took the initiative in many areas of mobilization: raising regiments, equipping them with arms and uniforms, providing help for the families of soldiers, organizing war production, supply and transportation, building coastal defenses, and so on. It now seems clear that rather than hindering the efforts of the government in Richmond, the activities of states augmented such efforts. "On balance," concludes a recent study of this question, "state contributions to the war effort far outweighed any unnecessary diversion of resources to local defense."[9]

As for the "died of democracy" thesis, a good case can be made that, to the contrary, the Confederate government enforced the draft, suppressed dissent, and suspended civil liberties and democratic rights at least as thoroughly as did the

Union government. The Confederacy enacted conscription a year before the Union, and raised a larger portion of its troops by drafting than did the North. And while Abraham Lincoln possessed more authority to suspend the writ of *habeas corpus* and used this power more often to arrest anti-war activists than did Jefferson Davis, the Confederate army suppressed unionists with more ruthlessness, especially in east Tennessee and western North Carolina, than Union forces wielded against Copperheads in the North or Confederate sympathizers in the border states.

This points to a second problem with the internal conflict interpretation; we might term this flaw the "fallacy of reversibility." That is, if the North had lost the war—which came close to happening on more than one occasion—the same thesis of internal conflict could be advanced to explain *northern* defeat. Bitter division and dissent existed in the North over conscription, taxes, suspension of *habeas corpus,* martial law—and significantly, in the case of the North, over emancipation of the slaves as a war aim. If anything, the opposition was more powerful and effective in the North than in the South. Lincoln endured greater vilification than Davis during much of the war. And Lincoln had to face a campaign for re-election in the midst of the most crucial military operations of the war—an election that for a time it appeared he would lose, an outcome that would have constituted a repudiation of his policy of war to victory and might have led to peace negotiations with an independent Confederacy. This did not happen, but its narrow avoidance is evidence of intense conflict within the *northern* polity—which tended to neutralize the similar but perhaps less divisive conflicts within the South as a cause of Confederate defeat.

Finally, we might ask whether the internal conflicts between state governments and central government or among different factions and leaders were greater in the Confederacy than they had been in the United States during the Revolution. Americans in the war of 1776 were more divided than southerners in the war of 1861, yet the United States won its independence and the Confederacy did not. Apparently we must look elsewhere for an explanation of Confederate failure.

Similar criticisms apply to another interpretation that overlaps the internal conflict thesis. This one might be termed the "internal alienation" argument. In recent years a great deal of scholarship has focused on two large groups in the Confederacy that were or became alienated from the war effort: nonslaveholding whites, and slaves. The nonslaveholders constituted two-thirds of the Confederacy's white population. Many of them, especially in mountainous and upcountry regions of small farms and few slaves, opposed secession in 1861. They formed significant enclaves of unionism in western Virginia where they created a new Union state, in east Tennessee, where they carried out guerrilla operations against the Confederacy and contributed many soldiers to the Union army; and elsewhere in the upland South. Other yeoman farmers who supported the Confederacy at the outset, and fought for it, became alienated over time because of disastrous inflation, shortages of food and salt, high taxes, and a growing conviction that they were risking their lives and property in a war to defend slavery. Clauses in the conscription law that allowed those who could afford it to buy a substitute and exempted from the draft one white man on every plantation with twenty or more slaves lent force to the bitter cry that it was a rich man's war but a poor man's fight. Many soldiers' families suffered severe hardship and malnutrition as food shortages and inflation worsened. Bread riots occurred in parts of the South during 1863—most notably in Richmond itself. Numerous soldiers deserted from the army to return home and support their families. Several historians have argued that this seriously weakened the Confederate war effort and brought eventual defeat.

The alienation of many southern whites was matched by the alienation of a large portion of that two-fifths of the southern population that was black and slave. Slaves were essential to the Confederate war effort. They provided a majority of the labor force. They made it possible for the South to mobilize three-quarters of its white men of military age into the armed forces—compared with about half in the North. Thus slavery was at one level a source of strength to the Confederacy. But at another level it was a source of weakness. Most slaves who reflected on their stake in the war believed that a northern victory would bring freedom. Tens of thousands voted with their feet for the Union by escaping to Yankee lines, where the North converted their labor power and eventually their military manpower into a Union asset. This leakage of labor from the Confederacy and the unrest of slaves who remained behind retarded southern economic efficiency and output. It also drained manpower from the Confederate army by keeping some white men at home to control the increasingly restless slave population.

The alienation of these two large blocs of the southern people seems therefore a plausible explanation for Confederate defeat. But some caveats are in order. The alienated elements of the American population during the Revolution were probably larger than in the South during the Civil War.

Many slaves ran away to the British, while the Loyalist whites undoubtedly weakened the American cause more than the disaffected nonslaveholders weakened the Confederate cause. Yet the Americans triumphed and the Confederates did not. It is easy to exaggerate the amount of class conflict and yeoman alienation in the Confederacy; some historians have done just that. And while large numbers of slaves ran off to Union lines, this happened only where Union military and naval forces invaded and controlled Confederate territory—which introduces an *external* factor and a possible alternative explanation for Union victory.

But perhaps the most important weakness of the internal alienation thesis is that same fallacy of reversibility mentioned earlier. Large blocs of northern people were bitterly, aggressively alienated from the Lincoln administration's war policies. Their opposition weakened and at times threatened to paralyze the Union war effort. Perhaps one-third of the border-state whites actively supported the Confederacy while many of the remainder were at best lukewarm unionists, especially after emancipation became a Republican war aim. Guerrilla warfare behind Union lines in these pro-Confederate regions occurred on a far larger scale than in the unionist areas behind Confederate lines. In the free states themselves, the Democratic party denounced conscription, emancipation, certain war taxes, the suspension of *habeas corpus,* and other measures to mobilize men and resources for an all-out war effort. Democrats exploited these issues in a relentless attempt to cripple the Lincoln administration. The peace wing of the party, the so-called Copperheads, opposed the war itself as a means of restoring the Union.

If the South had its class conflict over the theme of a rich man's war and poor man's fight, so did the North. (It does not matter whether it really was disproportionately a poor man's fight—I have argued elsewhere that it was not[10]—the important thing was the perception of class favoritism in the draft.) If the Confederacy had its bread riots, the Union had its draft riots, which were much more violent and threatening. If many soldiers deserted from Confederate armies, a similarly large percentage deserted from Union armies until the autumn of 1864, when the Confederate rate increased because of a perception that the war was lost and further sacrifice was useless. Note here that this rising southern desertion rate was primarily a *result* of defeat, not a cause. If the South had its slaves who wanted Yankee victory and freedom, the North had its Democrats and border-state unionists who strongly opposed emancipation and withheld their support from the war because of it. Thus internal alienation provides no more of a sufficient explanation for Confederate defeat than internal conflict, because the similar and probably greater alienation within the North neutralized this factor.

Another internal explanation for Confederate defeat has been around for a long time and has recently resurfaced in a number of studies. This one can be described as the "lack of will" thesis. It holds that the Confederacy could have won if the southern people had possessed the determination, the *will* to make the sacrifices and the total effort necessary to achieve victory. The most straightforward, unvarnished expression of this thesis was offered by E. Merton Coulter, a southerner, in his book *The Confederate States of America,* published in 1950. The South lost the war, said Coulter, because its "people did not will hard enough and long enough to win." In 1986 the four authors of *Why the South Lost the Civil War* echoed this conclusion: "We contend that lack of will constituted the decisive deficiency in the Confederate arsenal."[11]

Three principal themes have emerged in this lack-of-will thesis. First is an argument that the Confederacy lacked a strong sense of nationalism. The Confederate States of America, in this interpretation, did not exist long enough to give its people that mystical faith we call nationalism, or patriotism. Southerners did not have as firm a conviction of fighting for a country, a flag, a deep-rooted political and cultural tradition, as northerners did. Southerners had been Americans before they became Confederates, and many of them—especially former Whigs—had opposed secession. So when the going got tough, their residual Americanism re-emerged and triumphed over their newly minted glossy Confederate nationalism.

Proponents of the lack-of-will thesis point to the Confederate Constitution, which in most respects was a verbatim copy of the United States Constitution. The Confederate national flag was red, white, and blue with an arrangement of stars and bars not far different from the stars and stripes of the American flag. The great seal of the Confederacy portrayed George Washington, while Confederate money and postage stamps bore the portraits of Washington, Thomas Jefferson, Andrew Jackson, and other heroes of the American pantheon. Surely this indicates that Confederates were closet Americans subconsciously yearning to return to their old allegiance.

But this argument misses the point. Confederates regarded themselves as the true heirs of American nationalism, custodians of the ideals for which their forefathers of 1776 had fought. It was the *Yankees* who had repudiated these ideals. When the Black Republicans took over the government, southerners departed to form a new government that would conserve the genuine heritage of the old America. Confederate nationalism was American nationalism purified of malign Yankee domination. That is why Confederate money and stamps portrayed great Americans; that is why the Confederate Constitution retained most provisions of the United States Constitution. The South, said Jefferson Davis in his first message to the Confederate Congress after Fort Sumter, was fighting for the same "just course" of self-government that their revolutionary fathers had fought for. "Thank God! we have a country at last," said Mississippian L. Q. C. Lamar in 1861, a country "to live for, to pray for, to fight for, and if necessary, to die for."[12]

If the rhetoric of Confederate nationalism did not contain as many references to abstract symbols or concepts like flag, country, Constitution, and democracy as did Union rhetoric, southerners felt a much stronger and more visceral commitment to defending land, home, and family from invasion by "Yankee vandals." In this sense, Confederate nationalism was if anything stronger than its Union counterpart. In their letters and diaries, southerners expressed a fiercer patriotism, a more passionate dedication to "the Cause," a greater determination to "die in the last ditch" than northerners did. As the Confederate War Department clerk John Jones expressed it in his diary in 1863, the southern people had far more at stake in the war than northerners. "Our men *must* prevail in combat, or lose their property, country, freedom, everything. . . . On the other hand, the enemy, in yielding the contest, may retire into their own country, and possess everything they enjoyed before the war began." A Union officer who was captured in the battle of Atlanta on July 22, 1864, and spent the rest of the war in southern prisons, wrote in his diary on October 4 that from what he had seen in the South "the End of the War . . . is some time hence as the Idea of the Rebs giving up until they are completely subdued is all Moonshine they submit to privations that would not be believed unless seen."[13] Without question, the southern people persisted through far greater hardships and suffering than northern people experienced. Northerners almost threw in the towel in the summer of 1864 because of casualty rates that southerners had endured for more than two years. In the light of this, it seems difficult to accept the thesis of lack of will stemming from weak nationalism as a cause of Confederate defeat.

A second theme in the lack-of-will interpretation is what might be termed the "guilt thesis"—the suggestion that many southern whites felt moral qualms about slavery which undermined their will to win a war fought to preserve slavery. The South, wrote historian Kenneth M. Stampp, suffered from a "weakness of morale" caused by "widespread doubts and apprehensions about the validity of the Confederate cause." Defeat rewarded these guilt-ridden southerners with "a way to rid themselves of the moral burden of slavery," so a good many of them "perhaps unconsciously, welcomed . . . defeat." Other historians with a bent for social science concepts agree that Confederate morale suffered from the "cognitive dissonance" set up in their psyches by fighting a war to establish their own liberty but at the same time to keep four million black people in slavery.[14]

Historians who want to believe that southern whites felt guilty about slavery find this thesis attractive. But most of the evidence for it would seem to exist in the imaginations of these historians. To be sure, one can find quotations from southern whites expressing doubts or qualms about slavery. And one can find statements by southerners after the war expressing relief that it was gone. But the latter are somewhat suspect in their sincerity. And in any case one can find far more quotations on the other side—assertions that slavery was a positive good, the best labor system and the best system of social relations between a superior and inferior race. Two recent studies of former slaveowners after emancipation have concluded, in the words of one of them, that "nothing in the postwar behavior and attitudes of these people suggested that the ownership of slaves had necessarily compromised their values or tortured their consciences."[15]

In any case, most Confederates did not think of themselves as fighting for slavery but for independence. If slavery weakened southern morale to the point of causing defeat, should it not have weakened American morale in the Revolution of 1776 even more? After all Americans of that generation felt considerably more guilt about slavery than did southerners of 1861. And it is hard to see that Robert E. Lee, for example, who did have doubts and reservations about slavery—and about secession for that matter—made a lesser contribution to Confederate victory than, say, Braxton Bragg, who believed firmly in both slavery and secession.

A third theme in the lack-of-will interpretation focuses on religion. Southerners were a religious people; under the stress of suffering and death during the war they became more religious. At the outset, southern clergymen preached that God was on the side of the Confederacy. But as the war went on and the South suffered so much death and destruction, so much disaster and defeat, some southerners began to wonder whether God was on their side after all. Perhaps, on the contrary, he was punishing them for their sins. "Can we believe in the justice of Providence," asked one prominent Confederate, "or must we conclude that we are after all wrong?"[16] Several historians have pointed to these religious doubts as a source of defeatism and loss of will that corroded Confederate morale and contributed to southern defeat.

Notice the phrase "loss of will" in the preceding sentence. Not *lack,* but *loss.* There is a difference—a significant difference. A people at war whose armies are destroyed or captured, whose railroads are wrecked, factories and cities burned, ports seized, countryside occupied, and crops laid waste quite naturally lose their will to continue the fight because they have lost the means to do so. That is what happened to the Confederacy. If one analyzes carefully the lack-of-will thesis as it is spelled out in several studies, it becomes clear that what the authors are really writing about is loss of the will to carry on, not an initial *lack* of will. The book *Why the South Lost the Civil War,* which builds its interpretation around the *lack*-of-will thesis, abounds with *loss*-of-will phraseology: Union naval and military victories "contributed to the *dissolution* of Confederate power and will . . . *created* war weariness and *destroyed* morale. . . . The loss of Atlanta and Sherman's march, combined with Lincoln's re-election, severely *crippled* Confederate will to win. . . . By 1865 the Confederacy had *lost* its will for sacrifice." (Italics added)[17]

This is the right way to put it. It places the cause-effect relationship in the correct order—military defeat caused loss of will, not vice versa. It introduces external agency as a crucial explanatory factor—the agency of northern military success, especially in the eight months after August 1864. The main defect of the *lack*-of-will thesis, as well as of the internal conflict and internal alienation thesis discussed earlier, is that they attribute Confederate defeat to factors intrinsic to the South. Like the analysts of Confederate mistakes at Gettysburg, they tend to forget about the Yankees. Thus the four authors of *Why the South Lost* conclude flatly, in the face of much of their own evidence, that "the Confederacy succumbed to internal rather than external causes."[18]

This brings us back to the overwhelming-numbers-and-resources interpretation, which at least had the merit of recognizing the large external aspect of Confederate defeat. But the deficiencies of that interpretation remain. Another category of analysis with an external dimension, though, might seem to resolve the dilemma of explanation. This one focuses on leadership. Numerous historians both northern and southern—and British as well, for they have paid a lot of attention to the American Civil War—have argued that the North developed superior leadership which became the main factor in ultimate Union victory. This has produced a large and rich literature, which can only be briefly summarized here. It deals mainly with three levels of leadership.

First, generalship. A fairly broad consensus exists that the Confederacy benefited from better generalship in the first half of the war, particularly in the eastern theater and at the tactical level. But by 1864 a group of generals including Grant, Sherman, and Sheridan had emerged to top commands in the North with a firm grasp of the need for coordinated offensives in all theaters, a concept of the total-war strategy necessary to win this conflict, the skill to carry out the strategy, and the relentless, even ruthless determination to keep pressing it despite a high cost in casualties until the South surrendered unconditionally. In this interpretation the Confederacy had brilliant tactical leaders like Lee, Jackson, Forrest, and others who also showed strategic talent in limited theaters. But the South had no generals who rose to the level of overall strategic genius demonstrated by Grant and Sherman. Lee's strategic vision was limited to the Virginia theater, where his influence concentrated Confederate resources at the expense of the western theaters, where the Confederacy suffered from poor generalship and where it really lost the war.

The second level where a number of historians have identified superior northern leadership is in management of military supply and logistics. In Secretary of War Edwin M. Stanton, Quartermaster-General Montgomery Meigs, Assistant Secretary of the Navy Gustavus Fox, the administrators of military railroads Daniel McCallum and Herman Haupt, and numerous other officials the North developed by 1862 a group of top- and middle-level managers who organized the northern economy and the logistical flow of supplies and transportation to Union armies with unprecedented efficiency and abundance. The Confederacy could not match northern skill in organization and administration. Nor did the South manage its economy as well as the North. While the Union developed a balanced system of taxation, loans, and treasury notes to finance the war without unreasonable inflation, the Confederacy relied mostly on fiat money and suffered a crippling 9,000 percent inflation by war's end. In this interpretation, it was not the North's greater resources but its better management of those resources that won the war.

Third, leadership at the top. Lincoln proved to be a better commander in chief than Davis. On this there has been virtual unanimity among historians of northern birth, and surprising agreement by many southerners. A couple of quotations from two historians, one northern and one southern, writing sixty years apart, will give the flavor of this interpretation. The Yankee James Ford Rhodes wrote at the beginning of the twentieth century that "the preponderating asset of the North proved to be Lincoln." And in 1960 the southern-born historian David Potter put it even more strongly: "If the Union and the Confederacy had exchanged presidents with one another, the Confederacy might have won its independence."[19]

This may be carrying a good point too far. In any event, a broad consensus exists that Lincoln was more eloquent than Davis in expressing war aims, more successful in communicating with the people, more skillful as a political leader in keeping factions working together for the war effort, better able to endure criticism and work with his critics to achieve a common goal. Lincoln was flexible, pragmatic, with a sense of humor to smooth relationships and help him survive the stress of his job; Davis was austere, rigid, humorless, with the type of personality that readily made enemies. Lincoln had a strong physical constitution; Davis suffered ill health and was frequently prostrated by sickness. Lincoln picked good administrative subordinates (with some exceptions) and knew how to delegate authority to them; Davis went through five secretaries of war in four years; he spent a great deal of time and energy on petty administrative details that he should have left to subordinates. A disputatious man, Davis sometimes seemed to prefer winning an argument to winning the war; Lincoln was happy to lose an argument if it would help win the war. Davis's well-known feuds with two of the Confederacy's premier generals, Beauregard and Joseph E. Johnston, undoubtedly hurt the South's war effort.

The thesis of superior northern leadership seems more convincing than other explanations for Union victory. And yet—and yet—it should not be uncritically accepted. Some caution is advisable. With respect to generalship, for example, comparisons of Grant and Lee, Sheridan and Forrest, Sherman and Johnston, and so on, are a minefield through which historians had better maneuver carefully. And even if the North did enjoy an advantage in this respect during the last year or two of the war, the Union army had its faint-hearts and blunderers, its McClellan and Pope and Burnside and Hooker who nearly lost the war to superior Confederate leadership in the east in 1862–63, despite what was happening in the West. On more than one occasion the outcome seemed to hang in the balance because of *incompetent* northern military leadership.

As for Union superiority in the management of supply and logistics, this was probably true in most respects. Northern society was more entrepreneurial and business-oriented than southern society; the Union war effort could draw on a wider field of talent to mobilize men, resources, technology, industry, and transportation. Yet the Confederacy could boast some brilliant successes in this area of leadership. Ordnance Chief Josiah Gorgas almost literally turned plowshares into swords, building from scratch an arms and ammunition industry that kept Confederate armies better supplied than had seemed possible at the outset. The Rains brothers George and Gabriel accomplished miracles in the establishment of nitrate works, the manufacture of gunpowder, and the development of explosive mines (then called torpedoes), which turned out to be the Confederacy's most potent naval weapon. What seems most significant about Confederate logistics and supply is not the obvious deficiencies in railroads and the commissariat, to cite two notorious examples, but the ability of southern officials to do so much with so little. Instead of losing the war, their efforts did much to keep the Confederacy fighting for so long.

Finally, what about Lincoln's superiority to Davis as commander in chief? This might seem indisputable. Yet Lincoln made mistakes as a war leader. He went through a half-dozen failures as commanders in the eastern theater before he found the right general. Some of his other military appointments and strategic decisions could justly be criticized. And as late as the summer of 1864, when the war seemed to be going badly for the North, when Grant's forces had suffered horrendous casualties to achieve a stalemate at Petersburg and Sherman seemed equally stalemated before Atlanta, Lincoln came under enormous pressure to negotiate peace with the Confederacy. To have done so would have been tantamount to admitting northern defeat. Lincoln resisted this pressure, but at what appeared to be the cost of his re-election to the presidency. If the election had been held in August 1864 instead of November, Lincoln would have lost. He would thus have gone down in history as an also ran, a loser unequal to the challenge of the greatest crisis in the American experience. And Jefferson Davis might have gone down in history as the great leader of a war of independence, the architect of a new nation, the George Washington of the southern Confederacy.

This did not happen, but only because of events on the battlefield—principally Sherman's capture of Atlanta, and Sheridan's spectacular victories over Jubal Early in the Shenandoah Valley. These turned northern opinion from deepest despair in the summer to confident determination by November. In July, Horace Greeley had written to Lincoln pleading with him to open peace negotiations with the Confederacy. "Our bleeding, bankrupt, almost dying country," said Greeley, "longs for peace—shudders at the prospect of fresh conscriptions, of further wholesale devastations, and of new rivers of human blood." A month later the veteran Republican politician Thurlow Weed said that "the people are wild for peace. . . . Lincoln's reelection [is] an impossibility."[20] But less than two months later, after the fall of Atlanta and Sheridan's first two victories in the Shenandoah Valley, a British war correspondent expressed astonishment at the "extent and depth" of northern "determination . . . to fight it to the last. . . . They are in earnest in a way the like of which the world never saw before, silently, calmly, but desperately in earnest."[21]

This transformation of northern will illustrates the point made earlier that the will of either the northern or southern people was primarily a result of military victory rather than a cause of it. Events on the battlefield might have gone the other way, on these and other occasions during the war. If they had done so the course of the war might have been quite different. It is this element of contingency that is missing from generalizations about the cause of Confederate defeat, whether such generalizations focus on external or internal factors. There was nothing inevitable about northern victory in the Civil War. Nor was Sherman's capture of Atlanta any more inevitable than, say, McClellan's capture of Richmond in June 1862 had been. There were several major turning points, points of contingency when events moved in one direction but could well have moved in another. Two have just been mentioned:

Sherman's capture of Atlanta and McClellan's failure to capture Richmond. The former, coupled with Sheridan's success in the Shenandoah Valley, proved to be the final decisive turning point toward Union victory. Two earlier moments of contingency that turned in favor of the North were of equal importance.

The first occurred in the fall of 1862. Confederate offensives during the summer had taken southern armies from their backs to the wall in Mississippi and Virginia almost to the Ohio River and across the Potomac River by September. This was the most ambitious Confederate effort to win European recognition and a victorious peace on Union soil. But, in September and October, Union armies stopped these Confederate invaders at Antietam and Perryville. This forestalled European intervention, dissuaded northern voters from repudiating the Lincoln administration by electing a Democratic House of Representatives in the fall of 1862, and gave Lincoln the occasion to issue the Emancipation Proclamation, which enlarged the scope and purpose of the war.

The other major turning point came in the summer of 1863. Before then, during the months between Union defeats at Fredericksburg and Chancellorsville, a time that also witnessed Union failures in the western theater, northern morale dropped to its lowest point in the war—except perhaps during August 1864. The usually indomitable Captain Oliver Wendell Holmes, Jr., recovering from the second of three wounds he received in the war, wrote during the winter of 1862–63 that "the Army is tired with its hard and its terrible experience. . . . I've pretty much made up my mind that the South have achieved their independence." Even that staunch patriot Joseph Medill, editor of the *Chicago Tribune,* wrote in early

1863 that an armistice had to come: "The rebs can't be conquered by the present machinery."[22]

But then came the battle of Gettysburg and the capture of Vicksburg. This crucial turning point produced southern cries of despair. At the end of July, Confederate Ordnance Chief Josiah Gorgas wrote:

> One brief month ago we were apparently at the point of success. Lee was in Pennsylvania. . . . Vicksburgh seemed to laugh all Grant's efforts to scorn. . . . Now the picture is just as sombre as it was bright then. . . . It seems incredible that human power could effect such a change in so brief a space. Yesterday we rode on the pinnacle of success—today absolute ruin seems to be our portion. The Confederacy totters to its destruction.[23]

Predictions in July 1863 of the Confederacy's imminent collapse turned out to be premature. More twists and turns marked the road to the end of the war. This only underscores the point about the importance of contingency. To understand why the South lost, in the end, we must turn from large generalizations that imply inevitability and study instead the contingency that hung over each military campaign, each battle, each election, each decision during the war. When we comprehend what happened in these events, how it happened, why it happened, and what its consequences were, then we will be on our way toward answering the question: Why did the Confederacy lose the war?

2

Military Means, Political Ends: Strategy

ARCHER JONES

ANY ESTIMATE OF the role of strategy in the outcome of the Civil War would necessarily involve giving strategy a broad definition, one going beyond strictly military concerns to include such important and interrelated topics as diplomacy, economic mobilization, and finance. But to do this would make strategy too broad to provide a focused perspective on the war, one which would clearly illuminate the contribution of military strategy to victory and defeat.

Nevertheless, military strategy has such a close relation to the war's political objectives and concerns that any intelligible treatment must show its links to politics. Further, it is convenient to distinguish between military and political strategy by defining the former as military action designed to deplete the hostile military force and the latter as military action intended to produce a political result directly. Yet military and political strategy rarely have such clear-cut boundaries because most military actions have political effects. Thus northern and southern strategists had to consider the political effect of their military actions on not only the enemy but on the attitudes of foreign powers and the opinions of their own people, including the citizen soldiers. The attitude of the public had great importance in this war, the first large-scale, prolonged conflict between democratically organized countries in the age of mass circulation newspapers and widespread literacy.

The first Union strategic plan, a political strategy offered in the spring of 1861 by General in Chief Winfield Scott, proposed to use the pressure of a blockade and a campaign to control the Mississippi River to induce the seceded states to return to the Union. Though its elements became part of Union military strategy, it failed to promote a compromise. The failure of political strategy meant the North had to rely on military strategy. With a two to one numerical superiority of uniformed men, the Union armies, some foresaw, would gain a quick victory. And this would have happened had the tactical offensive had as much strength as the defensive and pursuit more speed than retreat. Under these circumstances Union armies could have defeated the Confederates in battle and then followed, overtaken, and beaten them over and over until they had depleted Confederate military forces and won the war. But, as had been true in western Europe for centuries, the opposite conditions actually prevailed, with the tactical defensive proving stronger than the offensive and retreat faster than pursuit. Thus generals commanding the weaker forces usually had a choice between fighting and withdrawing, and if they elected to fight they could do so in a strong position and face to face with their adversaries.

So the traditional ascendancy of the strategic defensive guaranteed that the North would face a long, hard task in trying to deplete an enemy equal in combat quality while invading a hostile country big enough to provide the Rebel armies with ample opportunities for retreat. Moreover, the Federals faced supply difficulties unknown to western Europe because the thinly populated South did not produce enough food to feed the huge northern armies unless they could remain in motion. This meant that, unless on the move and finding new supplies, the invaders had to rely on rations brought by river and railroad to supplement what they could find in the country. With smaller armies, the Confederates had fewer difficulties and, when they retreated, would leave behind for the Yankees a country denuded of supplies and railroads in need of repair.

Most Federal generals understood the dominance of the tactical and strategic defensive and recognized that they had only limited opportunities to deplete Rebel armies through combat. This led them to the tacit decision to seek to conquer the South's territory as the means of weakening its armies. The loss of control of territory would deprive the southern armies not only of their food and other production but of the manpower the lost area would have provided for the armies. Thus implicitly the Union generals rejected a combat strategy for wearing down the Rebels and adopted a logistic strategy of diminishing their armies by reducing their base for supply. Old, like most strategic ideas, this went back beyond ancient times. Julius Caesar, distinguishing between a logistic and a combat strategy, said he preferred "conquering the foe by hunger rather than by steel."[1]

The Confederacy explicitly understood the military menace presented by such a logistic strategy when President Jefferson Davis pointed out that the "general truth that power is increased by the concentration of an army is, under our peculiar circumstances, subject to modification" because the "evacuation of any portion of territory involves not only the loss of supplies, but in every instance has been attended by a greater or less loss of troops."[2]

Both governments also recognized the political significance of the gain and loss of territory because these provided a measure of military success and failure. This sign of achievement or discomfiture could affect the attitude of European powers and public opinion in both the North and South. Federal military victory could have played a part in a strategy which aimed at compromise and early reconciliation, and Confederate triumphs could have helped their initial strategy of gaining a quick victory through the intervention of European powers. The South had confidently expected that, when British textile factories stopped when the war cut off the supply of southern cotton, the British government would intercede to aid the South and so ensure its independence.

When "King Cotton" failed to bring intervention, the Rebels increasingly looked to the effect of their military actions on northern public opinion. They believed that a resolute and successful resistance could convince a majority of Yankees that victory would cost more in money, time, hardship, and casualties than saving the Union was worth. Increasingly, Confederate leaders and people, including the soldiers, looked to the Union presidential election of 1864 as the crucial time when the North could have a referendum on whether or not to continue the war. And Confederate leaders were also aware of the effect of military operations on their own people and on their estimation of whether the price of independence seemed too high. But the six-year Confederate presidential term precluded as early a southern referendum on the war.

Acutely aware of the influence of military events on northern public opinion, President Lincoln also found himself caught between the professional soldiers' views of military reality and the civilian perspective, which tended to see war almost exclusively in terms of battles. So the populace demanded battles from generals when most of them realized the ineffectiveness of a combat strategy. By the fall of 1862, Lincoln had come to understand the intrinsic indecisiveness of military operations but knew no way to interpret that to the people or to explain warfare in terms of the logistics and strategy of campaigns instead of succession of battles that rarely did more than produce short retreats by the defeated.

So the military strategy for both sides had to respond to political as well as military considerations. For the Union this created some tension because the slow working of a logistic strategy implemented by territorial conquest would have less appeal and inspire less popular confidence than a combat strategy, which concentrated on winning battles. Yet such a disregard of the primacy of the defensive could well have resulted not only in too many lost battles but in depleting the northern armies at a higher rate than the southern forces.

On the other hand, in defending against the Union's logistic strategy by giving priority to territorial defense, President Davis also pursued the political strategy which would have the best chance of discouraging the North. Moreover, maintaining the Confederacy's territorial integrity had an important effect on southern morale. In fact, it is doubtful that, in spite of its obvious merit, the Confederacy could have adopted a military strategy of employing deep withdrawals—the public would have responded to the retreats by becoming discouraged about the prospect of gaining independence at a reasonable cost.

The kind of military strategy needed to conquer territory can appropriately have the name persisting. This contrasted with the even older raiding strategy, which aims at accomplishing its military or political objective through a transitory presence in the hostile country. To fight to gain and retain control of enemy territory, soldiers used an operational strategy to guide army movements. That employed by northern and southern generals came from the wars of the French Revolution and Napoleon. With their proximity in time to the Civil War comparable to that of World War II and the 1990s, these wars had the same popular appeal as that which the World War has in the 1990s. In addition to the history of the campaigns, readers could find military writers who explained the principles underlying Napoleon's success. The most prominent of these, Antoine-Henri Jomini, a general in the French and then the Russian army, provided a foundation for the other authors. His 1838 *Summary of the Art of War,* available in English in 1854, brought together all of his ideas in succinct form, but readers needed a good knowledge of Napoleon's campaigns in order to understand the points he made. There is not much evidence to support the thesis that he had a broad influence on Civil War soldiers and none that the ideas he propounded antedated and were antithetical to Napoleon's practice.

Napoleonic strategy depended on rapid maneuvers with armies dispersing to move quickly or to find, confuse, or engage the enemy; the armies concentrated to fight. Much of this power of maneuver depended on the division, a unit of 3,000 to 8,000 men, able to fight independently because it usually included artillery and cavalry as well as infantry. Army commanders maneuvered divisions whose generals marched and fought with their infantry brigades and artillery and cavalry units.

From dispersal to cover a wide area or to deceive the enemy, Napoleonic strategy used concentration to bring superior force against the enemy. If a general found his adversary divided, he would try to concentrate most of his men against one part. The other basic Napoleonic maneuver occurred when a general succeeded in taking all or part of his army into the enemy's rear. The Civil War soldiers called this a turning movement, using the same term for this strategic maneuver as for the comparable tactical move.

The generals did not start as masters of the Napoleonic art of war but engaged in a course of self-teaching and emulation of good models presented by their fellow generals, enemy as well as friendly. Thus the campaigns of the war displayed an increasing sophistication in operational strategy. Nevertheless, the first campaign of the war showed many of the elements that would characterize the war's subsequent operations.

In July 1861 the North had political motives in inaugurating the campaign of the Battle of Manassas—to respond to the popular desire for military action and to drive back the Rebel army of General G. T. Beauregard in northern Virginia, almost insolently close to Washington. So, in July 1861, General in Chief Scott ordered forward General Irvin McDowell's army of 30,000 green troops stationed in Washington. Well aware that General J. E. Johnston's Confederate army in the Shenandoah Valley, less than 100 miles west of Washington, could reinforce Beauregard, Scott intended the Union army of Scott's opponent, General Robert Patterson, to keep Johnston occupied. Patterson failed. When McDowell began his advance and Beauregard telegraphed for aid, President Davis ordered Johnston to reinforce Beauregard. This he did, moving part of the way by railroad and arriving in time to give the Rebels a slight numerical superiority in the battle and help defeat McDowell's well-conceived attack.

Because the two Confederate armies were closer together than the Union armies of Patterson and McDowell, they could have won any race to concentrate on the Manassas battlefield, a situation for the southern forces which Jomini had called interior lines. In this campaign the Confederates had used the telegraph and the railroad to apply Napoleon's strategy of concentrating dispersed forces; this use of the products of the industrial revolution to expand the application of Napoleonic strategy would characterize the Civil War and become a particular feature of Rebel strategy.

By defeating the Union's strategic goal of driving them back, the Confederates won the campaign. Yet many have criticized them for not pursuing their beaten foe. But, as disorganized by victory as the Federal army by defeat, they could do little to overtake their retreating adversary or take the strategic and tactical offensive, cross the Potomac River, and capture Washington.

In the form of casualties, campaigns have tactical as well as strategic results. The casualties, or manpower depletion, of each army are a byproduct of any combat, even that which implemented a logistic rather than a combat strategy. The best measure of this bit-by-bit depletion, or attrition, is to state it as a percentage of the combatants' total forces. In the battle and campaign of Manassas the defeated Federals lost 9 percent, the victorious Rebels less than 7 percent, of their army. In the political domain this campaign heartened the Rebels and discouraged the Yankees; yet, by showing many in the North that their armies could not win quickly, doubtless it conferred some benefits.

The essentially political objective of driving back the Rebel army near Washington, now commanded by J. E. Johnston, remained the Union strategy in Virginia. Well aware of the superiority of the tactical and strategic defense, McDowell's successor, General George B. McClellan, had no desire to attempt to advance directly on Johnston's army. Instead, he planned to use the fine communications provided by the Chesapeake Bay and Virginia's rivers to carry out a strategic turning movement. Since to reach the rear of the Confederate army near Washington required surprising Johnston, something McClellan could not achieve, the Union general settled for a landing at the tip of the Peninsula between the James and York rivers and an advance up the Peninsula to the vicinity of Richmond. This move would draw Johnston's army away from Washington to defend Richmond, thus accomplishing the minimum strategic objective of the campaign.

Moreover, McClellan could advance up the Peninsula without serious frontal combat because Union command of the rivers would enable him to force Johnston back by the threat of landing troops in his rear. The Union general believed that his approach to Richmond would so threaten the Confederates that they would attack to drive him away, giving him the advantage of the tactical defensive.

All went according to McClellan's plan, his army reaching the vicinity of Richmond in May 1862. Johnston then lashed out at him in the Battle of Fair Oaks. McClellan's men repulsed the attacks and inflicted on the Rebels the loss of 6,000 killed, wounded, and missing, suffering 5,000 casualties themselves. This gave them a victory of attrition, McClellan losing 5 percent of his 100,000 men, Johnston 10 percent of his 60,000. An even broader and more pertinent measure made a still more favorable comparison. Since all Union forces outnumbered the Confederates by at least two to one, the southern losses, as a percentage of total troops available, amounted to more than double the Union's.

Thus McClellan's strategy had worked as intended. And, by repulsing the attack, the general had gained the strategic success of maintaining his threatening position. Because the defeated Rebels did not retreat, however, they deprived the Yankee army of this essential symbol of victory and, consequently, of much of its political effect in either the South or North.

When a wound dictated Johnston's replacement, President Davis gave the army to General R. E. Lee. The new commander, who also subscribed to the thesis that McClellan's army could capture Richmond by a siege, saw its presence as a serious political embarrassment and wished to recover the valuable farming areas given up to Union occupation because of McClellan's advance. Moreover, Richmond, as a major industrial center, had great logistic importance. In late June, after concentrating troops at Richmond, Lee attempted to drive McClellan back by turning him. But, since the turning force arrived a day late, the Confederates made only frontal attacks. McClellan responded by withdrawing his army to the James River, an excellent alternate supply line. In pursuing the Union army, the Confederates made more attacks, giving the name Seven Days' Battles to the conflict. In this battle McClellan gained a tactical victory in terms of attrition, suffering fewer than 16,000 casualties to the Rebels' more than 20,000, meaning that the South's percentage loss was again more than double the North's. In pushing the Federal army away from Richmond, the Confederates had attained only their minimum strategic goal, but the victory, signalized by McClellan's retreat, had a positive effect in the South and quite a negative one in the North.

In assessing the Seven Days' Battles, President Lincoln noted the political "importance to us, for its bearing upon Europe, that we should achieve military successes; and the same is true for us at home as well as abroad." He also knew that his army had won a tactical victory because he realized that "in men and material, the enemy suffered more than we," and "is less able to bear it." So he found it frustrating that such a "half-defeat should hurt us so much" in "moral effect."[3] But for the public, which army retreated determined the victory; and to many, battles seemed the essence of warfare.

Before McClellan began his Peninsula campaign in March 1862, General H. W. Halleck, the Union commander in Missouri and West Tennessee, had already made a dramatic advance. With no major political objective, he launched a military operation designed to drive the Rebels from southern Kentucky and the western half of Tennessee and take control of the Mississippi River as far south as Memphis, Tennessee. Halleck could conduct such an ambitious campaign in spite of the tremendous obstacle of the winter mud because he could move in steamers on the western rivers and had the support of a U.S. Navy gunboat flotilla. The Ohio, Mississippi, Tennessee, and Cumberland rivers all interconnected and all but the Ohio served as routes of invasion for Halleck's forces.

Anticipating just such an advance, the Confederates had built forts on the banks of the rivers and armed them with heavy guns to prevent the passage of even armored gunboats. These forts could stop gunboats but could not cope with the troops that Halleck sent with them in steamers. In February 1862, Halleck dispatched 15,000 men under General U. S. Grant up the Tennessee, escorted by Flag Officer Andrew H. Foote's flotilla. Following Halleck's directions, Grant landed near Fort Henry and sent part of his army to turn it. Before the Union force could reach the fort's rear, the Confederate garrison escaped and marched eastward a few miles to join the garrison of Fort Donelson on the Cumberland River.

Grant then marched after them and, coming up behind Fort Donelson, immediately surrounded it while drawing from the river supplies and reinforcements sent by Halleck. Cut off and its huge garrison inadequately supplied, the fort surrendered. Instead of emulating Jefferson Davis's prompt action to concentrate against McDowell in the Manassas campaign, the Rebel commander, A. S. Johnston, had failed to use his rivers and railways to concentrate his forces against Grant. Instead, when Fort Henry fell, he acknowledged defeat by abandoning Kentucky but reinforcing Fort Donelson with enough men to add a tactical disaster to the strategic defeat. Then, seeing Union forces on the Tennessee River turning their positions and those on the Cumberland able to do the same, the Confederates evacuated Nashville and their strongest fort on the Mississippi.

In less than three weeks Halleck, Grant, and Foote had

demolished the whole Confederate position, taken thousands of square miles of fertile farming country, and captured the important commercial and industrial center of Nashville—a major triumph for the North's logistic strategy. And they had won an important victory of attrition, for Grant in taking Fort Donelson had suffered 3,800 casualties but had inflicted 16,600 on the enemy, mostly in prisoners. The dramatic advance and the fall of the fort had enhanced northern morale and had a negative effect on southern expectations for an early victory.

Yet the swift and unexpected catastrophe transformed Confederate command behavior. A. S. Johnston and General Beauregard, his new second in command, used the railroad to concentrate most of Johnston's forces at Corinth, a railway junction in northern Mississippi. President Davis made an equally emphatic response in also ordering to Corinth a small force from Charleston, South Carolina, substantial numbers from New Orleans, and General Braxton Bragg and most of his men from the Gulf coast. These forces moved rapidly by railroad and steamer. Relying largely on the telegraph and steam, the Confederate command made a concentration which, by including troops from the Atlantic and Gulf coasts and Arkansas, had a truly national scope, the kind of concentration which Napoleon, depending on human and animal mobility only, had employed only within a single theatre of war. With this concentration they planned a counterattack to recover some of the immense logistic and political losses of February. They aimed to strike Grant, halted on the Mississippi River about 20 miles north of Corinth, before he could receive the reinforcement of General D. C. Buell's army, ordered by Halleck from Nashville to march to his aid.

On April 6, just as McClellan began moving on the Peninsula, A. S. Johnston began the Battle of Shiloh with a surprise assault on Grant's army. But, reinforced by Buell, Grant repelled the attack in a two-day battle in which Johnston died. In failing to recover lost ground, the Confederates suffered another strategic defeat and, in losing 10,600 men to Grant's and Buell's 13,000, suffered another tactical setback of attrition. The northern criticism of Grant for allowing the Rebels to surprise him diluted the victory's positive effect in the North.

Halleck then assumed personal command of the armies of Grant and Buell, took Corinth, ordered Buell eastward to take Chattanooga, and then went to Washington to become Union general in chief. Here he arrived in time to try to cope with a different type of Confederate offensive.

The Seven Days' Battles having caused casualties of more than 20 percent of the large southern army, Davis and Lee had agreed on the need for a less costly form of counterattack. In abandoning the idea of offensive battles, their new approach resembled McClellan's strategy. Lee stated it succinctly as a policy of "not attacking them in their strong and chosen positions. They ought always to be turned."[4] Like McClellan's strategy, Lee's aimed not to reach the enemy's rear so much as to compel his retreat by the threat of doing so. He demonstrated it in his campaign against General John Pope's Federal army covering Washington.

In making the orthodox move of using his interior lines to concentrate against Pope, Lee planned "to avoid a general engagement" and only oblige Pope to retreat "by manoeuvering." In this way he would attain the basic logistical objective of his new style of counterattacking, to recover the "beef, flour, & forage" of the area north of Richmond.[5] To conduct his turning movement Lee sent half of his force under General T. J. Jackson to Pope's rear, where it destroyed the railroad and supply depot at Manassas and then withdrew westward to leave Pope a clear route of retreat to Washington. Thus Lee implemented his concept of the defensive turning movement to force the enemy back without battle.

But Pope made an unsuccessful frontal attack on Jackson on the old battlefield of Manassas. The next day, when the other half of Lee's army arrived on Pope's flank, the Union general had to retreat to Washington. But at 9,000 losses, compared with Pope's 16,000, Lee had avoided a consequential tactical defeat of attrition. Moreover he gained his strategic objective and secured a splendid victory, which encouraged the Rebels and dismayed many Yankees.

Lee immediately adapted his new turning strategy to deal with his always pressing supply problems by deciding to cross the Potomac well to the west of Washington with the idea of spending the fall in Maryland, his army dining on the recent harvest there while his quartermasters and commissaries brought in the Virginia harvest to carry his army through the winter. Unlike his just-completed campaign of the Second Battle of Manassas, an application of persisting strategy, his move into Maryland could not give him permanent occupation of his position there. With only a limited area of control and without rail connections to the Confederacy, he was carrying out a raid, which meant that he could have only a temporary presence, departing in the late fall after a fine period of living at the enemy's expense.

But his ability to do this depended on the enemy, and Lee apparently thought that McClellan's traditional caution and deliberateness in preparation and movements would mean a long time before he advanced. Returned from the Peninsula and commanding his and Pope's armies, McClellan began moving toward Lee with unaccustomed celerity and accelerated when he captured Lee's plans. The campaign had the essentially political objective of driving the Rebels back to Virginia.

In mid-September, ten days after McClellan left Washington, Lee received his attack in the Battle of Antietam. In a costly defensive battle, the Confederates succeeded in fending off the clumsy attacks of the large Federal army. But, concentrated to fight, Lee could not forage to feed his raiding army. McClellan, on the other hand, had access to a railroad which enabled him to supply his men while they remained poised to fight the Rebels again. Thus Lee's success in resisting McClellan's attacks, a tactical victory in battle, did not alter the need to retreat to Virginia, a move Lee made after waiting a day to prove he had won the battle.

Since the political definition of losing is retreat, Lee had lost the battle. Since he would have had to withdraw after any battle, his decision to fight assured a negative political result in the South and a positive one in the North. The battle, and Lee's retreat, provided Lincoln with the opportunity to make his politically significant Preliminary Emancipation Proclamation and may even have forestalled British diplomatic intervention. Had McClellan been unwise enough to retreat when his attacks failed, Lee would still have had to withdraw because he could not disperse to forage in the presence of a large Union army under McClellan, or his successor, who doubtless would have responded to the northern political need by making a renewed advance on Lee. So strategically and politically Lee's Antietam campaign was a fiasco. It was really doomed to fail, but Lee could have mitigated the political damage by ending his raid without a battle. The Confederate capture of a large Federal garrison made the loss ratio in the campaign essentially neutral.

While Lee deliberately combined the raid with the turning movement, General Braxton Bragg conducted a campaign into Kentucky which he converted into a raid when he could not complete the classic turning movement. Assuming command in northern Mississippi, Bragg immediately moved half of his army by rail south to Mobile, Alabama, and then north through Atlanta to Chattanooga. Here, in conjunction with General Edmund Kirby Smith's Confederates in East Tennessee, he advanced northward, passing east of the flank of General Buell, who based his army on Nashville and the railroad, to Louisville. It looked as if he might succeed in turning Buell and recovering Middle Tennessee.

Seeing himself turned, Buell began moving north along the Louisville and Nashville Railroad. But Bragg kept ahead of him and when, in southern Kentucky, he established his army on Buell's railroad and blocked his retreat, Bragg had completely turned Buell. The Confederate general, realizing that his strategic offensive with the turning movement had given him the advantage of the tactical defensive in the coming battle, ordered his army to begin digging entrenchments to strengthen its defense. But Buell declined to fight a battle, and with ample supplies in depots along his railroad he could afford to wait. But Bragg could not tarry in an area of low agricultural productivity while remaining concentrated to block Buell. Thus thwarted by Buell's better supply situation, Bragg converted his invasion into a raid by moving off the railroad and marching northwest to join Kirby Smith in the fertile Blue Grass region of central Kentucky.

Buell promptly marched north to Louisville, incorporated reinforcements into his army, and moved into central Kentucky to drive Bragg out. After an inconclusive battle at Perryville, Bragg realized that he could not face Buell who could supply himself by means of the railroads from Louisville and Cincinnati. So he and Kirby Smith retreated by the route through eastern Kentucky and eastern Tennessee by which Kirby Smith had come.

Bragg's spectacular raid raised and then dashed Rebel expectations. The public did not realize that, as Lee had in the Antietam campaign, Bragg had made a raiding rather than a persisting advance. Thus they expected the Confederate troops to hold central Kentucky. It also proved a political failure in that Kentuckians disappointed the Confederates' expectations that many would volunteer for the Rebel army. In terms of its minimum strategic objective, to remove the threat to Chattanooga, Bragg had succeeded when he established his army only about 30 miles southeast of Nashville. The campaign suffered no adverse attrition.

Even before the Kentucky and Antietam campaigns, raiders had already had a decisive influence on operations in the West. In spite of overwhelming numbers, Buell had failed to take Chattanooga in July and August of 1862. He owed his defeat to the disabling of his supply lines largely by raids conducted by Confederate cavalry which broke his railroad in Kentucky as well as Tennessee. They easily wrecked a railroad by taking up rails and, especially, by burning the wooden bridges and trestles which so often carried the tracks.

In this work the regular cavalry had effective assistance

from southern guerrillas, quite active in Middle Tennessee. Here they controlled the countryside through intimidating the Union supporters in the country by burning houses and beating or killing people. They proved adept raiders of vulnerable railways, often moving through familiar country at night to shift a rail or burn a bridge.

Both guerrillas and regular cavalry could take advantage of the offensive superiority of the raid over the persisting defense that tried to interdict movements into Union territory, protect hundreds of miles of railroad, and intercept the raiders. The raid gained its dominance over the defense by its ability to exploit retreat's advantage over pursuit, and the ambiguity of the raiders' movements. With the intruders' wide choice of objectives and routes, defenders did not know where to head off their incursion and, if successful, would find their adversary retreating rather than fighting. The raiders' ability to withdraw by a different route than that of their advance gave the defenders an equally difficult task to intercept retreat. In their raids, guerrillas could use an additional mode of retreat when they ended their raid by blending in with the civilian population.

When the effectiveness of the raid and the strength of the guerrillas had required Buell to use two divisions to guard his communications and control the occupied areas, he had made a representative Union defensive commitment. As the northern armies moved beyond the rivers which had provided secure as well as efficient transportation, they had to commit a third of their forces to defending their communications, thus weakening their main armies which were striving to conquer Confederate territory.

In their war against the guerrillas, Federal troops emulated their adversary in using intimidation, often not pausing to try a captive before killing him. They used reprisals, like burning farms and even villages, but their most effective means in Middle Tennessee proved to be a version of the traditional hostage technique. By taking the property of wealthy citizens when a guerrilla raid occurred nearby, they convinced them to use their considerable influence to make the guerrillas desist. Arming local Unionists also had excellent results, one Union officer noting that these local forces, who knew and hated their Rebel enemies, were "killing many of the worst men in this part of the state and will soon drive the guerrillas out." Toward the end of the war a Union officer could report from Middle Tennessee that a "most distinguishing feature in this country . . . is the manner in which these people are cowed by the force of the Govt."[6]

Coping with Rebel raids had fully occupied Halleck's first three months as general in chief. He then turned his attention to implementing for December 1862 simultaneous advances of all the main armies east of the Mississippi. Though operations had usually occurred at the same time in east and west, Halleck's effort amounted to something of an innovation. Simultaneous advances, that is, concentration in time, could counter the Confederate concentration in space, practiced on a national scale in the Shiloh campaign. Thus, by engaging every Rebel army at the same time, concentration in time could nullify concentration in space.

The first move occurred in Virginia, where McClellan's successor, General Ambrose E. Burnside, marched from northern Virginia toward Richmond, drawing Lee after him to halt Burnside and repulse his inept attack at the Battle of Fredericksburg on December 13. Although Burnside's advance recovered some territory, the battle losses contributed nothing to attrition and had a negative effect on the northern perception of the likelihood of a victory at a reasonable cost.

In Mississippi, Grant advanced down the railroad to turn and capture Vicksburg, the most important of the two remaining Confederate strongholds on the Mississippi. But he had not gone far when Rebel cavalry raids broke his railroad and destroyed his depot. Deprived of supplies, he withdrew just as General William T. Sherman led an expedition down the river to the city. After an essentially hopeless attack against fortifications, Sherman also fell back. These defeats, coming about without big battles or consequential attrition, amounted to a significant political defeat, and not merely because of the effect on the morale of the two publics. Vicksburg itself had little military importance, the Confederacy having negligible trade between its two halves and the North losing only a modest transportation advantage from its inability to use the river. But control of the historically important river would be a major symbol for both sides, sustaining the North in its quest for victory and making many more southerners doubtful of the possibility of independence at a reasonable cost.

At the end of December, Buell's successor, General William S. Rosecrans, marched against Bragg to destroy him in battle. Predictably, he failed but, with equal losses, gained a victory of attrition and, by Bragg's 20-mile retreat, brought the northern public very welcome relief from the gloom of the successive defeats in December.

By early 1863, Halleck and Lincoln had completed their formulation of Union strategy. Not abandoning concentration in time but assigning priority to objectives, they placed their main emphasis on opening the Mississippi, adding an advance up river to Grant's augmented downstream effort. Second, to complete the conquest of Tennessee and open the way to Georgia, they strengthened the forces operating against Tennessee with an army corps from Virginia. In Virginia they accepted the stalemate which the year's operations had shown existed there. Moreover, Halleck was certain that a siege of Richmond would not only fail to take the city but would enable the fortified Confederates so to economize on men as to transfer troops to other theatres. Since the Rebels at Fredericksburg were 50 miles from Washington, keeping Lee at this barely acceptable political distance from the northern capital became the main objective for the army in Virginia. Lincoln also insisted on trying to hurt Lee's army by catching him in a mistake or conducting a compaign aimed at harming him.

In the spring of 1863 the Confederate secretary of war asked Lee whether he could spare some men to reinforce Tennessee. Lee, faced with the conflict between his knowledge of strategy and his desire not to lose any men, responded with a variety of arguments against giving up any troops. He also included the suggestion that he could help Tennessee more by making another raid like his Antietam campaign. This exchange with the Secretary has helped some to see Lee as attempting to win the war with his army in Virginia, or, overlooking the defensive character of his strategy and the three defensive battles since the Seven Days' Battles, as pursuing the unrealistic strategy of trying to annihilate the enemy in battle.

Happily for an understanding of his strategy at this time, he gave his wife a clear statement of the basic Confederate political strategy and his means of implementing it. Of the strategy for dealing with the Yankees, he wrote: "If we can baffle them in their various designs this year & our people are true to our cause . . . , I think our success will be certain." Trusting soon to have his "supplies on a firm basis," he continued: "On every other point we are strong. If successful this year, next fall there will be a great change in public opinion at the North. The Republicans will be destroyed & I think the friends of peace will become so strong as that the next administration will go in on that basis. We have only therefore to resist manfully."[7] Clearly he had so far succeeded in baffling the enemy, and resisting manfully did not include an attempt to destroy the enemy in battle or try to win the war with offensive action.

After an initial effort by Burnside had bogged down in the winter mud, at the end of April, Burnside's successor, General Joseph Hooker, attempted to hurt Lee with a good plan to turn him. But Hooker did not act with sufficient vigor at the Battle of Chancellorsville and Lee turned his turning movement; ultimately the Union general withdrew. Though he had heavy losses, he achieved some favorable attrition, but the battle and the retreat affected the publics in the usual way.

At the same time, the navy ferried Grant's army east across the Mississippi, enabling him to avoid vulnerable railroad communications and to turn Vicksburg from below. He then marched to the city's rear and bottled it up. Moreover, he captured an army of nearly 30,000 in the city, making it a victory in terms of casualties as well as a major political triumph. This opening of the Mississippi had a profound effect by spreading hope in the North for an early victory and in the South widespread pessimism.

Meanwhile, Lee had repeated his Antietam campaign on a more ambitious scale, advancing into southern Pennsylvania. Neither he nor President Davis intended this campaign to have any effect on the siege of Vicksburg. In addition to having a logistical motive, as earlier, Lee also wished to avoid again defending near Fredericksburg and having to fight a costly battle to protect his valuable supply area north of Richmond. If, on the other hand, he fought a battle in Pennsylvania, he could choose his position and compel the Union army to fight another battle of Fredericksburg. But again Lee overlooked the political effect of fighting. Even a victorious defensive battle would look like a defeat because of the inevitable retreat of a raiding army forced to concentrate and unable to forage.

The campaign followed its predictable course, giving the Confederacy the strategic success of living at the enemy's expense while crops matured in Virginia. But, instead of a Battle of Fredericksburg, Lee, attempting to exploit what he mistakenly believed was a serious Union dispersal, attacked the army of Hooker's successor, General George G. Meade, and suffered a costly defeat in a three-day battle at Gettysburg. In losing perhaps as many as 28,000 men to the North's 23,000, the battle became a disaster of depletion for the Confederate army, and his inevitable retreat to Virginia, seemingly the result of the battle rather than his inability to forage, made it a serious political defeat also.

One could reasonably expect the South to have abandoned the war when confronted with the loss of the Mississippi, the consequent symbolic separation of the country, and Lee's failure in Pennsylvania in a campaign which to many people seemed a bid to win the war by invading the North. But the

South continued its burdensome struggle for independence. Increasingly southerners looked to the 1864 elections in the North when they hoped that their steadfast resistance would have convinced the voters that restoring the Union was not worth the cost of the apparently endless war.

While Grant awaited Vicksburg's surrender and Lee marched to Gettysburg, Rosecrans, a convert to the turning movement, displayed an exceptional mastery when he turned Bragg back to the Tennessee at a cost of only 600 casualties. In August he moved again and gained another bloodless strategic victory, this time crossing the Tennessee River and turning Bragg out of Chattanooga and back into north Georgia.

But this victory triggered a long-contemplated Confederate concentration against Rosecrans's army. Essentially reenacting the Shiloh concentration, the Confederate command brought troops to northern Georgia from East Tennessee and Mississippi and sent two divisions from Lee's army. With these forces Bragg counterattacked at the Battle of Chickamauga, driving the Federal army into Chattanooga and besieging it there. This counteroffensive had the strategic merit of driving Union forces out of northern Georgia. The victory had the expected political impact of inspiriting the Confederates and discouraging the North. But losing over 18,000 to the Union's 16,000 men made it a serious tactical defeat of attrition. The casualties suffered in this counterattack illustrate a cost of the Confederacy's logistically important and politically essential strategy of defending its territorial integrity.

It had taken the Union armies 19 months from the capture of Nashville in February 1862 to the fall of Chattanooga to advance along the 100 miles of railroad between the cities, a line surrounded by guerrillas and vulnerable to cavalry raiders. Grant and his friend and collaborator William T. Sherman knew the difficulties of implementing Union strategy, because, in taking Vicksburg they had faced a Confederate general who had equal numbers. Although Grant had twice as many men as the Confederates, he had committed half to holding West Tennessee and northern Mississippi and protecting their railroads from guerrilla and cavalry raids.

During the early winter of 1863–64, Grant completed the formulation of a new strategy, one in which the Union would give up its reliance on the persisting strategy of territorial conquest but still pursue its logistic strategy of crippling the Rebel armies by depriving them of their supply base. Instead of a persisting strategy he would use raids to break the southern railroads and thus isolate the armies from the farms, factories, foundries, and ports that sustained them. Rather than using cavalry, he planned to rely primarily on infantry armies which had the manpower to do a thorough job of destruction. The armies would also live at Rebel expense and destroy agricultural and industrial resources as well as railroads.

By changing to raids, the Union would shift to a strategy in which the offensive dominated the defensive. Exploiting the ambiguity of the raiders' objectives and routes of advance and withdrawal, large armies could penetrate the South and do great damage as they moved through. Grant planned three such raids: one for the winter from southeastern Virginia through North Carolina would break the two railroads to Virginia and end with the capture of the port of Wilmington; another, for the spring and using troops from west of the Mississippi, would land to capture the port of Mobile, Alabama, and march inland to destroy the railroads and threaten Atlanta; and the third raid, originating in northern Georgia, would begin after the capture of Atlanta and go to the Atlantic or Gulf coast, breaking Georgia's railroads on the way to the coast.

In February, Sherman demonstrated the new strategy when he led 21,000 men, mostly infantry, on a 300-mile round trip march from Vicksburg to Meridian, Mississippi, to destroy the railroads, warehouses, and works. In wrecking 115 miles of track and destroying 61 bridges, he exhibited the raid's effectiveness in implementing a logistic strategy.

Even though Grant became general in chief in March 1864, no raid opened the spring campaign of 1864. Lincoln and Halleck had refused to order the winter North Carolina raid, and Sherman, commanding the army in northern Georgia, had to take Atlanta first, a more difficult task because the troops were not ready for the Mobile raid. So the 1864 campaign followed the usual pattern of simultaneous Union advances in east and west, with Grant directing Meade in Virginia and Sherman moving on Atlanta. Grant aimed to keep Lee so occupied that he could not emulate the Chickamauga campaign by sending men to help oppose Sherman. Although Grant had hopes of capturing Richmond by cutting its communications from the rear or reaching them after he had turned Lee back to the city, the essence of his strategy lay in Sherman's taking Atlanta and beginning his raid.

But the people in the North and South had their attention focused not on Sherman but on Virginia, where Grant would face Lee. This put great pressure on Grant to win battles to meet popular expectations, especially in the year of such a crucial election. In his campaign he usually fought Lee prior to turning him, and he had made a very serious effort to defeat him at Spotsylvania. Secretary of War Stanton gave publicity to these battles and to the subsequent turning movements as pursuits of the vanquished. But the conflicts occurred so close together and each cost so many casualties that many people, confronted by appalling losses in a short time, did not see the battles as victories, nor believe that the Rebels had lost more men, nor accept that Grant needed to amass such casualties just to push Lee back. When the campaign ended in June, the army had begun to besiege Petersburg, 25 miles south of Richmond and a key to its communications but neither an impressive ending for the campaign nor a fair recompense for the loss of 70,000 men. Grant's campaign thus constituted an encouragement for the South and a political liability for Lincoln, whose re-election chances it hurt, especially as the likely Democratic nominee was General McClellan, whose 1862 campaign had reached a comparable strategic position with negligible casualties. Actually Lee had suffered about half of Grant's losses, thus giving the Union only a slight victory of attrition.

Meanwhile, using the minimum of combat, Sherman methodically turned his adversary back toward Atlanta, moving slowly as he repaired, fortified, and garrisoned the railroad in his rear. Sherman did not complete his last turning movement into Atlanta's rear and take the city until September 1. Though a major victory for and the last application of the old persisting logistic strategy, the fall of Atlanta, a manufacturing and railroad center, had far more political than military importance. The northern public celebrated it as a sign that the Union could win the war in a reasonable time. It thus aided the election on Lincoln, though continuation of the conflict seemed not to depend on him because General McClellan, as the Democratic nominee, had declared that he would accept no peace without reunion. Yet the re-election of Lincoln gave much emphasis to the North's determination and so dashed southern hopes more than McClellan's declaration. The brother of Confederate Vice President A. H. Stephens thus estimated the effect of the defeat of northern peace advocates on southerners' confidence in victory at a bearable cost: "It has been sustained, and the collapse prevented even up to this time, only by the hopes which our people had from the peace party in the North."[8] When the peace party lost, confidence among southern citizens and soldiers dropped markedly. The significantly increased rate of desertion from the Rebel armies illustrated this.

So the war showed signs of drawing to a close before Grant could apply his innovative strategy. Sherman had delayed beginning his raid, because, after the fall of Atlanta, his opponent, General John B. Hood, first turned him back nearly to Tennessee and then marched away to menace Middle Tennessee and suffer defeat at Nashville. After reinforcing the Federal forces in Tennessee, Sherman abandoned Atlanta and began his raid in mid-November, taking a month to reach the Atlantic, where he captured Savannah and established a base. He had destroyed 200 miles of railroads and many cotton mills, took 7,000 horses, and, he reported, "consumed stores and provisions that were essential to Lee's and Hood's armies." Sherman had always been aware of the political significance of his raid and had viewed it not only as intimidation but as an evidence of Union victory, which would symbolize defeat for the Rebels. He expressed this idea when he wrote that "if the North can march an army right through the South, it is proof positive that the North can prevail in this contest."[9] Since Sherman's raid did persuade some southerners and strengthen the conviction of others that independence was costing more than its value, it constituted a significant political triumph as well as a major victory for the logistic strategy.

Sherman received Grant's authorization for a new raid into the Carolinas in the winter of 1865. At last able to carry out his full scheme of raids, Grant directed 40,000 men to Mobile for a raid into Alabama. Cavalry had a role too, when a large force from Tennessee struck the Alabama industrial center of Selma. The other major cavalry raid, which occurred in Virginia, northwest of Richmond, wrecked the canal along the James River as well as the railroads. Grant believed that this panoply of raids would "leave nothing for the Rebellion to stand upon."[10] Yet already, in the fall and early winter of 1864–65, some 40 percent of the Confederate soldiers east of the Mississippi deserted. So, before Grant's logistic raiding strategy of destruction of transportation, industrial, and agricultural resources could deplete the Confederate armies, they already were dwindling away because soldiers, like civilians, found the price of independence too high.

So, unlike the defeat of Germany in World War II, the Civil War did not end almost entirely as a result of military victory. The Confederate armies melted away not because men lacked supplies but because they and their families no longer had the political motivation to continue. Understood in these terms, what contribution did the military strategy make to victory and defeat?

The blockade, which, because it did not deny the South essential imports, failed to have a major military effect but did make a significant political contribution. It did this through accentuating the hardships of the war by reducing the southern standard of living and denying consumers enough of many of the imports, such as coffee, which they valued. This was a cost of war which northerners did not have to bear.

The strategy of the war on land had conscious political objectives and had the same harmony the blockade showed between military means and political needs. Choosing a logistic strategy because of the impracticality of the combat alternative, the Union had a strategy which, by conquering places, could give continual evidences of success to its soldiers and public.

Assuming that the Confederates were correct that the morale of their people required maintaining their territorial integrity and that discouraging the northern public needed this also, then the South pursued a politically as well as militarily wise strategy when it sought to protect its resources from conquest by Union armies. But this strategy involved much combat and, consequently, the wear on morale of heavier casualties than the alternative military strategy of less combat and of deep withdrawals. These would have exposed the Federal armies to profound logistical problems and the exhaustion of constant harassment by guerrillas. Yet, in addition to the political objection to sacrificing so much territory, this strategy could hardly have left slavery unaffected.

As far as acting to conciliate or intimidate the enemy, the Union armies generally kept themselves in harmony with political strategy, seeking to propitiate southerners, as well as such a destructive organization as an army could, and thus keeping in step with Lincoln's conciliatory reconstruction plan. It largely reserved intimidation for guerrillas, applied it effectively, and so cowed enemies that it could not conciliate.

The South made effective use of the cavalry raid against the invaders' railroads, thus exploiting the particular vulnerability of railroads and of armies dependent on bases. This, like guerrilla warfare, proved very effective and had no particular political impact. The defensive turning movement, best exemplified in Lee's Second Manassas campaign, was a valuable military innovation and fully in harmony with Confederate political goals. When combined with the raid and used once by Bragg and twice by Lee, it had the raid's traditional merit of living at the enemy's expense but, as used, had a negative political effect when combined with a battle prior to withdrawal. We cannot know whether, without the battles, people would still have seen such raids as defeated invasions. But clearly the battles presented a rare instance of such dissonance between military action and political goals.

Grant's raiding strategy, like the Confederate cavalry and guerrilla raids, aimed to exploit the vulnerability of railroads and of armies which depended on bases. When conducted like Sherman's to Meridian, in Georgia, and in the Carolinas, they had a favorable political impact because in the North they looked like victories and in the South, defeats. One can only wonder what would have happened if the Union had used them a year or more earlier. It is easy to speculate that their military and political effectiveness would have ended the war sooner and with fewer casualties.

Thus, for the most part, military strategy harmonized, and was made to harmonize, with political needs. In that neither belligerent outshone the other in its strategy, military strategy had a neutral effect in the war. But the similarity in strategy only occurred because enough soldiers on each side understood Napoleonic strategy and many displayed adaptability and innovativeness. Resemblance also stemmed from the role of public opinion, crucial for both belligerents, which meant that military campaigns often had to meet a double criteria for victory, the popular as well as the strategic. This interrelation of military events and strategy with public opinion reached a peak in the campaigns which preceded the crucial Union election of 1864. The attention both sides gave these campaigns shows how fully both military and civilian leaders understood the important connections between military means and political ends and shaped strategy accordingly.

3

"Upon their Success Hang Momentous Interests": Generals

GARY W. GALLAGHER

ANY ASSESSMENT OF the impact of generalship on the result of the Civil War must necessarily focus on three individuals. Admirers of some of the more than one thousand other men who achieved the rank of general in either the Union or Confederate armies might construe this as a slight to their heroes. After all, those officers helped organize the respective national armies and influenced individual campaigns and battles in myriad ways. But Ulysses S. Grant, Robert E. Lee, and William Tecumseh Sherman shaped military events to a far greater degree than any of their comrades. Grant and Sherman directed Federal offensives in 1862–65 that eventually destroyed the morale and capacity to resist among southern whites, while Lee's strategic and grand tactical skills more than once threatened to translate hopes for an independent Confederacy into reality. These three men made decisions that profoundly influenced events behind the lines and abroad as well as on the battlefield—indeed, it is impossible to discuss the reasons for northern victory or southern defeat without coming to terms with their dominant roles in the war. While some may disagree with the methods of Grant and Sherman, few contest their credentials as architects of Union victory. Lee's impact on Confederate fortunes remains more hotly debated, a circumstance that places him at the center of this essay.

Before examining Lee and other commanders, it is appropriate to note that current scholarship usually looks far from the battlefield to explain northern victory and hence treats generalship as largely irrelevant. Drew Gilpin Faust, for example, observed in a recent article on Confederate women that contemporary scholars "have answered the historiographical perennial, 'Why the South lost the Civil War,' by emphasizing deficiencies in Southern morale. Almost all such arguments stress the importance of class conflict, especially growing yeoman dissent, in undermining the Southern Cause." Faust accepts the validity of this line of approach but argues that the importance of gender has been overlooked. Portraying southern women as increasingly disenchanted with a war that vitiated the partriarchal compact, she concludes that in large measure the Confederacy "did not endure longer . . . because so many women did not want it to." Connections between Confederate military fortunes and the attitudes of women and male civilians scarcely intrude on Faust's analysis.[1]

Richard E. Beringer, Herman Hattaway, Archer Jones, and William N. Still, Jr., similarly played down the importance of campaigns and battles in their exhaustive *Why the South Lost the Civil War*. Easily the most detailed treatment of the subject, this book assessed the theories of several generations of historians before offering its own explanation for Confederate defeat. Like Faust, the authors of *Why the South Lost* pointed to disaffection behind the lines and concluded that "the Confederacy succumbed to internal rather than external causes." Wracked by doubts about slavery, alienated from a central government that repeatedly violated the doctrine of state rights to sustain its war effort, and unable to construct a viable nationalism, southern whites, "by thousands of individual decisions, abandoned the struggle for and allegiance to the Confederate States of America." The activities of armies and generals supply a violent backdrop against which the authors pursue their thesis, but only occasionally do military events move into the foreground as an important element in determining the state of morale behind the lines.[2]

The view that non-military factors largely explain Confederate defeat is not new. Historians such as Bell I. Wiley, Charles W. Ramsdell, E. Merton Coulter, and Kenneth M. Stampp have emphasized political, social, economic, and ideological influences that sapped civilian morale and thereby undermined southern resistance. A combination of these forces led to a situation in which, as Coulter put it, southern whites "did not will hard enough and long enough to win." As with many recent studies, military events frequently remained peripheral in the writings of these historians. Yet occasionally (and perhaps inadvertently) the direct link between home front and battlefield stood out boldly. An example of this phenomenon may be found in Wiley's *The Road to Appomattox,* a deft exploration of the reasons for Confederate defeat that allots minimal attention to the broader impact of military campaigns. Wiley included among the illustrations for his book a chart titled "Curve of Confederate Morale 1861–1865" which vividly connects military actions and the civilian front—with a single exception, the benchmark events on the chart are battles or campaigns. Southern morale peaked in July 1861 at the time of First Manassas, plunged in the spring of 1862 after repeated Confederate reverses in the western theater, then rebounded when Lee's army won dramatic victories at the Seven Days and Second Manassas. Except for a brief rise in late spring and early summer 1864 when Grant and Sherman bogged down in Virginia and Georgia, the chart follows a generally descending curve through 1863–64 and on to Appomattox.[3]

None of this is meant to deprecate the contributions of historians who have chosen to pursue lines of investigation apart from the military sphere. A collection of immensely complex and interrelated factors determined the outcome of the war, among which *was* an ultimate failure of will among southern whites behind the lines. But no shift in civilian morale North or South—and really none of the non-military factors—can be fully understood outside of the context of the military ebb and flow.

James M. McPherson aptly observed in *Battle Cry of Freedom,* "Defeat causes demoralization and loss of will; victory pumps up morale and the will to win." He pointed to the striking turnaround in northern attitudes in the late summer of 1864, when deep pessimism gave way to rampant optimism following Union victories at Mobile Bay and Atlanta. "The southern loss of will was a mirror image of this northern determination," added McPherson, and the "changes of mood were caused mainly by events on the battlefield." Testimony from participants underscores this point, none more dramatically than the entry for July 28, 1863, in Josiah Gorgas's diary. After watching developments along the Mississippi River and in Pennsylvania, the able chief of Confederate ordnance summed up his feelings in the wake of disasters at Gettysburg, Vicksburg, and Port Hudson: "Yesterday we rode on the pinnacle of success—today absolute ruin seems to be our portion. The Confederacy totters to its destruction." Across the Potomac in Washington, Commissioner of Public Buildings Benjamin Brown French had reacted to news of the Seven Days in comparable fashion about a year earlier. Looking through his journal on July 4, 1862, French was struck by "how long we have all been expecting that Richmond would be taken! And now the doings of the past week have driven back our immense army from within 4 miles of Richmond to 20! . . . Two or three such strategic movements would annihilate our army. . . . I now almost despair of our ever taking Richmond. . . ."[4]

This essay proceeds from the assumption that generals made a very great difference in determining the outcome of the war. Their actions decided events on the battlefield, which in turn either calmed or aggravated internal tensions that affected the ability of each government to prosecute the war. From a similar point of departure thirty years ago, T. Harry Williams explored Union and Confederate military leadership in an influential essay that postulated basic differences between the opposing generals. Williams found the key to these differences in the respective northern and southern responses to ideas put forward by Swiss military theorist Antoine-Henri Jomini. Obsessed with important cities or pieces of territory rather than the opponent's army, stated Williams, Jomini favored an earlier type of warfare free of ideology and wide-scale destruction beyond the battlefield. Jomini also advocated the offensive, stressing the importance of massed strength, interior lines, and safe avenues of advance; however, he shrank from the idea of campaigns of annihilation.

Williams asserted that northern generals such as George B. McClellan accepted Jomini's fixation with places and limited warfare, while their more daring southern counterparts such as Lee and "Stonewall" Jackson embraced his love of the offensive. All of these men failed "to grasp the vital relationship between war and statecraft," insisted Williams, and thus marked themselves as generals who looked to the past rather than to the future. They might win victories—Lee won a series of spectacular ones—but they lacked the vision to win a mighty struggle between two societies. Only with the emergence of Grant and Sherman did Civil War military leadership break free of Jominian shackles to anticipate modern warfare. These pre-eminent northern soldiers came to accept war against civilian populations as well as against enemy armies and recognized the importance of civilian psychology, thereby displaying an awareness of "the political nature of modern war." In doing so, thought Williams, they practiced their craft according to principles articulated by German theorist Carl von Clausewitz (though neither man had read his writings at the time of the Civil War) while also demonstrating their superiority over the hidebound Jominians on both sides of the Potomac.[5]

Herman Hattaway and Archer Jones challenged Williams's taxonomy of Civil War generalship in their imposing *How the North Won: A Military History of the Civil War*. They stressed that virtually all the leading officers on both sides shared common experiences, whether it was studying under the same professors and reading the same textbooks at West Point or learning the value of turning movements from Winfield Scott's impressive campaign to Mexico City in 1847. Almost to a man the generals recognized the tactical power of the defensive and in theory shunned frontal assaults except as a last resort. Acknowledging the difficulty of achieving decisive tactical results, they tended to concentrate on territory—Federals seeking to conquer the logistical heartland of the South; Confederates hoping to protect those same productive areas. "As might have been expected," commented Hattaway and Jones in summary, "in view of the common parentage of both armies, their respective leadership did not differ significantly in outlook and doctrine." With a few notable exceptions, "both sides conducted the war competently and realistically."[6]

Persuasive in refuting the notion of a dichotomous Jominian influence on most Civil War generals, Hattaway and Jones joined Williams in placing Grant, Lee, and Sherman in a special category. Williams asserted that in "the last analysis, the only Civil War generals who deserve to be ranked as great are Lee for the South and Grant and Sherman for the North"—and Lee's manifest gifts could not overcome his inability to transcend the purely military to confront the broader dimension of a modern war. Hattaway and Jones essentially agreed with this estimate: "Although in operational skill Lee stands out above all other army commanders, the major military contribution to victory remains the strategy of Grant." That strategy fulfilled "its logistical and political objectives" and with the capture of Atlanta inspirited northern civilians. Sherman fostered Union victory by adding a psychological dimension to his friend's grand strategy of exhaustion.

Northern armies in the final year of the conflict not only struck at the logistical underpinnings of the Confederacy but also sought to "produce a profound political impact by bringing the war home to all rebel states, thus exhibiting the inability of the Confederacy to protect its territorial integrity."[7]

Should students examing the reasons for northern triumph devote substantial attention to commanders beyond the obvious triumvirate? The potential value of studying the Ambrose E. Burnsides, Albert Sidney Johnstons, Joseph Hookers, and other more gifted generals is undeniable. Their many failures and occasional successes unquestionably affected morale in the ranks and among civilians back home. But if the campaigns of Grant, Lee, and Sherman are removed from the equation, performances at the top levels of command on each side translate into largely negative influences on the respective populations. They convey no sense of building momentum toward eventual victory. In fact, it is difficult to imagine a scenario within which any other Union or Confederate general could either formulate or implement a decisive strategy. The one exception is Winfield Scott, who possessed the intellectual capacity but lacked the physical stamina to undertake long-term direction of the Union war effort.

A rapid canvass of theater and army commanders underscores their inability to preside over a winning effort. Joseph E. Johnston and George B. McClellan never overcame their natural inclination to play it safe and hope for an essentially bloodless victory. Johnston always kept at least one eye fixed on lines of retreat; McClellan never exhausted his stock of excuses for failing to pursue outnumbered Rebel armies. Both men vastly underestimated civilian hunger for aggressive success on the battlefield. Braxton Bragg, Don Carlos Buell, and

William S. Rosecrans took turns fumbling opportunities for significant victories in Kentucky, Tennessee, and Georgia. Farther west, campaigning along the Mississippi River and elsewhere revealed the essential incompetence of John C. Pemberton and Nathaniel P. Banks, while P. G. T. Beauregard's fanciful strategic musings after 1862 had scant potential beyond their power to impress the parlor crowd in Richmond or Charleston. On a lower rung of proficiency, John Bell Hood, John Pope, and Benjamin F. Butler compiled records to challenge even the most fervent revisionist historian.

More impressive was Stonewall Jackson, who performed feats in the Shenandoah Valley and elsewhere that dazzled both friends and enemies. But Jackson never led a real army and proved sadly deficient in administrative and political acumen. Although the generalship of both Philip H. Sheridan and Jubal A. Early sometimes showed to advantage during campaigning in the Shenandoah Valley during the summer and fall of 1864, Sheridan's lopsided advantage in men and material masked severe shortcomings and Early suffered several tactical lapses and quarreled often with his cavalry officers and other subordinates. George H. Thomas surely possessed the skills to hold a position or smash a hopelessly outnumbered foe, yet his natural lethargy, among other attributes, limited his potential as an army commander. Finally, such generally competent officers as George G. Meade and Henry W. Halleck lacked the resolute strength of character and military vision to lead the way to final victory.

The spotlight must come back to Grant, Lee, and Sherman. In the century and a quarter since Appomattox, Grant's reputation has grown to the point where he usually is acknowledged as the greatest soldier of the war. J. F. C. Fuller foreshadowed much modern scholarship in a comparative study of Grant and Lee published in 1932. Remarking in his preface that he originally "accepted the conventional point of view that Grant was a butcher and *Lee* one of the greatest generals the world has ever seen," Fuller proceeded to construct a strong brief for Grant's superiority over his famous antagonist. He employed two sets of tables comparing losses in Grant's campaigns with those sustained by Lee's troops to refute the notion that Grant suffered inordinate casualties. Readily conceding Lee's many gifts as a commander, Fuller nonetheless found him incapable of growth and unable to comprehend the immense scope of the conflict. Fuller's overall conclusions conform closely to those of Williams and Hattaway and Jones: "[Grant] sees the war as a whole far more completely so than *Lee* ever saw it. His conceptions are simpler and less rigid; he is pre-eminently the grand-strategist, whilst *Lee* is pre-eminently the field strategian."[8]

This represented a dramatic shift from the long-dominant image of "Grant the Butcher." A standard element of Lost Cause explanations for Confederate defeat, the argument that an unimaginative but brutally determined Grant merely applied overwhelming resources to wear down Lee's army had worked its way into the broader literature long before Fuller wrote. Jubal Early, who ranked as the premier Lost Cause warrior, offered a classic example of this viewpoint in a lecture delivered on the anniversary of Lee's birth in 1872: "General Lee had not been conquered in battle, but surrendered because he had no longer an army with which to give battle. . . . [It] had been gradually worn down by the combined agencies of numbers, steam-power, railroads, mechanism, and all the resources of physical science." "Shall I compare General Lee to his successful antagonist?" asked Early rhetorically. "As well compare the great pyramid which rears its majestic proportions in the valley of the Nile, to a pigmy perched on Mount Atlas."[9]

Early's case against Grant depended on a simplistic reading of the 1864 Overland Campaign wherein the Federal commander seemed unable to envision any course but a straight-ahead bludgeoning of his more agile opponent. Absent from Early's work, as well as that of other writers who portrayed Grant as a butcher, was any detailed treatment of Grant's brilliant campaign against Vicksburg, his decisive success at Chattanooga, or his other western operations. Moreover, critics failed to grasp that Grant's tactics in 1864 went against his preferred style of campaigning. He fought Lee at every turn primarily because he wished to deny Jefferson Davis the option of shifting Confederate troops from Virginia to Georgia where they might slow Sherman's progress. Perhaps most unfair about many negative assessments of Grant was their implication that any clumsy slugger could have brought northern resources to bear against the Confederacy. As Richard N. Current observed three decades ago in his essay "God and the Strongest Battalions," the side with more men and matériel usually wins. Superior resources alone, however, cannot guarantee victory. The North always enjoyed a substantial edge in manpower and almost every manufacturing category, but none of Grant's predecessors proved equal to the task of harnessing and directing that latent strength. Grant's ability to do so stands as one of his greatest achievements.

A few critics continue to fight a rearguard action against Grant, but the historical consensus clearly recognizes his indispensable role as the architect of northern military victory. He brought rational direction and unshakable moral courage to his post as general in chief. Sherman best captured the latter quality when he told James Harrison Wilson in October 1864 that Grant "don't care a damn for what the enemy does out of his sight, but it scares me like hell! . . . He uses such information as he has according to his best judgment; he issues his orders and does his level best to carry them out without much reference to what is going on about him and, so far, experience seems to have fully justified him."[10] Grant's steady hand at the helm after March 1864 gave the North bright prospects for victory. There would be no failure of nerve at the front, no turning back because of temporary setbacks. If the northern public remained committed to victory, it had the commander in place to follow through in the field.

Sherman served as a superb agent of Grant's strategy of exhaustion. The failure of generals such as Nathaniel Banks, Ben Butler, and Franz Sigel to carry out their part of Grant's plan to apply simultaneous pressure at several vital points in the Confederacy made Sherman's role all the more important. As stated before, no officer understood better the immense psychological damage large-scale raids could inflict on civilians (and by extension on their relatives and neighbors in the southern armies). Russell F. Weigley has made the point that "it was Sherman much more than Grant who developed the implications of seeing the war as a contest between peoples beyond the contest of armies." During preparations to strike across Georgia from Atlanta to the Atlantic, Sherman revealed a sophisticated grasp of his operation's logistical, political, and psychological potential: "I propose to act in such a manner against the material resources of the South as utterly to negative [Jefferson] Davis' . . . promises of protection. If we can march a well-appointed army right through his territory, it is a demonstration to the world, foreign and domestic, that we have a power which Davis cannot resist." Sherman believed that such a march would be "proof positive" to southern whites that "the North can prevail in this contest, leaving only open the question of its willingness to use that power."[11]

The veteran Union army that swept across Georgia and then northward through the Carolinas accomplished everything Sherman asked of it. Apart from untold millions of dollars of property his soldiers destroyed, Sherman exposed the vulnerability of Confederate territory previously thought to be beyond the reach of northern arms. Just as Sherman predicted, the helplessness of Jefferson Davis's government left many Confederate civilians angry or dazed. "Last night came tidings of the fall of Savannah," wrote a North Carolina woman in her diary on December 27, 1864. "So fall all our hopes, all our boasts of 'crushing' Sherman. How empty they now seem!" Two days later this woman observed that "Sherman has effected a brilliant 'coup,' to march through the whole State of Geo, take its principal city & seaport in spite of our utmost endeavor, nay in our very teeth . . . with an army too which we proclaimed jaded and foot sore (but of whom he gives a very different account). It does indeed entitle him to pride & exultation." A refugee in South Carolina, shocked at the spectacle of Sherman's men pillaging and then burning the town of Barnwell, wrote simply: "I've no plans for the future."[12] Sherman's impressive campaign during late fall and winter 1864–65, together with the dreary stalemate and unrelenting casualties at Petersburg, delivered a body blow to

Confederate morale that set the stage for final northern victory.

Grant and Sherman thus formed a remarkable partnership perfectly suited to carry out Abraham Lincoln's national strategy during the last year of the war. Equally dedicated to crushing the rebellion, the president and his two generals pressed forward when northern hopes lagged during the bitter summer of 1864. Just as Grant's victories in Tennessee during 1862 and at Vicksburg and Chattanooga in 1863 had rallied northern morale at crucial moments, so also did his grand strategy bear fruit in time to resuscitate the Union war effort in September and October 1864. Military success bred political success, and neither would have been likely without the presence of Grant and Sherman.

The greatest obstacle to northern victory during the last year of the war, as it had been since June 1862, was R. E. Lee and his Army of Northern Virginia. Lee's transcendent reputation as a great captain remains firmly ensconced in the popular mind, and virtually no one challenges his brilliance as a field commander. But scholars increasingly have questioned his larger contribution to the Confederate war effort. Did he fail to see beyond his beloved Virginia, crippling Confederate strategic planning through a stubborn refusal to release troops badly needed elsewhere? Did his strategic and tactical choices lengthen the conflict, thereby increasing the odds that northern civilian morale would falter? Or did his penchant for the offensive unnecessarily bleed Confederate manpower when a defensive strategy punctuated by limited counteroffensives would have conserved southern resources? Did his celebrated victories improve the odds for Confederate nationhood, or were they nothing but gaudy sideshows that diverted attention from more significant military events elsewhere? In short, what was Lee's impact on the outcome of the war?

One of the most common criticisms of Lee alleges a lack of appreciation for the problems and importance of the trans-Appalachian Confederacy. J. F. C. Fuller frequently alluded to Lee's inability to see the war as a whole. The British author stated in one characteristic passage that Lee "was so obsessed by Viginia that he considered it the most important area of the Confederacy . . . . To him the Confederacy was but the base of Virginia."[13] A number of subsequent historians expanded upon the idea that Lee failed to take in the entire strategic situation. Especially strident in this regard was Thomas L. Connelly, who wondered "whether Lee possessed a sufficiently broad military mind to deal with over-all Confederate matters." Connelly saw Lee as intensely parochial, blinded by a desire to protect Richmond, and unwilling or unable to look beyond each immediate threat to his native state and its capital. When Lee did turn his attention to the West, averred Connelly, he invariably made suggestions "in the context of his strategy for Virginia." Connelly and Archer Jones reiterated many of these points in their study of Confederate command and strategy. They questioned Lee's knowledge about the geography of the West and deplored his habit of requesting reinforcements for the Army of Northern Virginia at the expense of other Confederate armies. Even Lee's grudging deployment of two-thirds of James Longstreet's First Corps to Georgia in September 1863 had a Virginia twist—he hoped that the movement might save Knoxville and shield Virginia's western flank.

Connelly and Jones admitted that all theater commanders tended to see their own region as most important but asserted that Lee's doing so proved especially harmful. He had been Davis's military adviser in the early days of the war and remained close to the president throughout the conflict; moreover, his reputation exceeded that of any other Confederate army commander. The result was as predictable as it was pernicious for the Confederacy: "His prestige as a winner and his unusual opportunity to advise undoubtedly to some degree influenced the government to take a narrower view on strategy and to go for the short gain in Virginia where victory seemed more possible." In the opinion of Connelly and Jones, Lee's influence was such that a powerful "Western Concentration Bloc," the roster of which included Joseph E. Johnston, P. G. T. Beauregard, James Longstreet, and John C. Breckinridge, could not counter his lone voice. The consequent failure to shift forces to threatened areas west of Virginia hindered the southern cause.[14]

Lee's aggressive style of generalship, with its attendant high casualties, also has generated much criticism. Grady McWhiney and Perry D. Jamieson propounded the thesis that a reckless devotion to offensive tactics bled the South "nearly to death in the first three years of the war" and sealed the fate of the Confederacy. Lee fit this pattern perfectly, they observed, sustaining losses approaching 20 percent in his first half-dozen battles compared with fewer than 15 percent for the Federals. A controversial aspect of McWhiney and Jamieson's book ascribed the South's love of direct assaults to a common Celtic ancestry. Whether or not readers accept the proposition that a cultural imperative prompted Lee to order attacks, McWhiney and Jamieson succeeded in accentuating his heavy losses throughout the war. Elsewhere, McWhiney bluntly claimed that the "aggressiveness of Robert E. Lee, the greatest Yankee killer of all time, cost the Confederacy dearly."[15]

A number of other historians agreed with McWhiney. The Army of Northern Virginia suffered more than 50,000 casualties in the three months after Lee assumed command, claimed Thomas L. Connelly, and over all "the South's largest field army, contained in the smallest war theater, was bled to death by Lee's offensive tactics." Russell F. Weigley asserted that Lee shared Napoleon's "passion for the strategy of annihilation and the climactic, decisive battle" and "destroyed in the end not the enemy armies, but his own." J. F. C. Fuller believed that Lee's only hope for success lay in emulating "the great Fabius," who often retreated to avoid costly battles. Instead, time and again Lee "rushed forth to find a battlefield" and "by his restless audacity, he ruined such strategy as his government created." Alan T. Nolan's reasoned analysis of Lee explored the question of "whether the general's actions related positively or negatively to the war objectives and national policy of his government." Nolan thought Lee came up far short when measured against this standard. His strategy and tactics won specific contests and made headlines but traded irreplaceable manpower for only fleeting advantage. "If one covets the haunting romance of the Lost Cause," wrote Nolan, "then the inflicting of casualties on the enemy, tactical victory in great battles, and audacity are enough." But such accomplishments did not bring the Confederacy closer to independence. Lee's relentless pursuit of the offensive contravened the strategy best calculated to win southern independence and thus "contributed to the loss of the Lost Cause."[16]

One last piece of testimony on this point typifies a common tension between admiration for Lee's generalship and a sense that his aggressive actions might have hurt the Confederacy. In a lecture delivered at a symposium on Lee in 1984,

Frank E. Vandiver commented that his subject "lost a lot of men by attacking and attacking and attacking" and "may have been too addicted to the offensive, even against outstanding firepower." Vandiver then quickly hedged his conclusion: "I think that you have to balance the fact that he lost a lot of men and stuck to the offensive against what he considered to be the strategic necessities of attack. So I would level the charge that he might have been too addicted to the offensive with some trepidation."[17]

These historians raise serious questions about the relationship between Lee's generalship and Confederate chances for independence. A different reading of the evidence, however, suggests that Lee pursued a strategy attuned to the expectations of most Confederate citizens and calculated to exert maximum influence on those who made policy in the North and in Europe. Far from being innocent of the importance of the West and the psychological dimension of his operations, he might have seen more clearly than any of his peers the best road to Confederate independence. His victories buoyed southern hopes when defeat lay in all other directions, dampened spirits in the North, and impressed European political leaders. They also propelled him to a position where, long before the end of the war, he stood unchallenged as a military hero and his Army of Northern Virginia had become synonymous with the Confederacy in the minds of many southern whites.[18] While his army remained in the field there was hope for victory; his capitulation extinguished such hope and in effect ended the war. Lee had selected a strategy that paradoxically enabled the Confederacy to resist for four years *and* guaranteed that it would not survive the surrender of his army at Appomattox.

Modern historians usually attribute Confederate military defeat to failure in the West, where vast chunks of territory and crucial cities fell to the Federals. They often add that Lee's unwillingness to send part of his own army to bolster forces beyond the Appalachians may have hastened Confederate defeat. Is this belief in the primacy of western campaigns a modern misreading of the actual situation? Certainly it was the Virginia theater that captivated foreign observers. For example, Lee's victories at the Seven Days and Second Manassas in the summer of 1862 conveyed to London and Paris a sense of impending Confederate success. Apparently unimpressed by the string of Union triumphs in the West extending from Fort Henry through the fall of New Orleans, Prime Minister Viscount Palmerston and Emperor Napoleon III leaned toward some type of intervention by the first week in September. Northern public opinion also seemed to give greater weight to the Seven Days than to events in Tennessee, prompting Lincoln's famous complaint to French Count Agénor-Etienne de Gasparin in early August: "Yet it seems unreasonable that a series of successes, extending through half-a-year, and clearing more than a hundred thousand square miles of country, should help us so little, while a single half-defeat should hurt us so much."[19]

Other evidence of a northern preoccupation with the East abounds. Albert Castel has noted that Lincoln himself, who beyond doubt believed the West to be more important, visited the Army of the Potomac several times but never favored a western army with his presence (Jefferson Davis joined his western armies on at least three occasions). Senator Charles Sumner revealed a good deal about attitudes among powerful northern politicians when he wrote during the winter of 1865 that Secretary of War Edwin M. Stanton thought "peace can be had only when Lee's army is beaten, captured or dispersed." Sumner had "for a long time been sanguine that, when Lee's army is out of the way, the whole Rebellion will disappear." So long as Lee remained active, "there is still hope for the Rebels, & the unionists of the South are afraid to show themselves."[20] Among the most telling indications of the public mood was a demand that Grant go east when he became general in chief of the Union armies in March 1864. He could have run the war as efficiently from Tennessee or Georgia, but the North wanted its best general to bring his talents to bear on the frustrating Virginia theater.

If anything, the South exhibited a more pronounced interest in the East. Following reverses in Tennessee and along the Mississippi River during the winter and spring of 1862, Confederates looked increasingly to Virginia for good news from the battlefield. Stonewall Jackson supplied it in the spring of 1862 with his Shenandoah Valley campaign—after that, Lee and the Army of Northern Virginia provided the only reliable counterpoint to northern gains in other theaters and consequently earned a special position in the minds of their fellow Confederates. "I feel thankful," wrote Georgian Mary Jones in the wake of Lee's triumph at Fredericksburg in December 1862, "that in this great struggle the head of our army is a noble son of Virginia, and worthy of the intimate relation in which he stands connected with our immortal Washington." Lamenting the fall of Vicksburg in late July 1863, Kate Stone, a young refugee in Texas, added, "Our only hope is in Lee the Invincible." Ten months and the reverse at Gettysburg did not alter Stone's thinking about Lee. "A great battle is rumored in Virginia," she wrote in May 1864,

"Grant's first fight in his 'On to Richmond.' He is opposed by the Invincible Lee, and so we are satisfied we won the victory." A Louisiana officer serving in the West echoed Stone's opinion on May 27, 1864, dismissing talk of a setback in Virginia with an expression of "complete faith in General Lee, who has never been known to suffer defeat, and probably never will."[21]

No one better illustrated the tendency to focus on Lee than Catherine Ann Devereux Edmondston of North Carolina. "What a position does he occupy—," she recorded in her diary on June 11, 1864, "the idol, the point of trust, of confidence & repose of thousands! How nobly has he won the confidence, the admiration of the nation . . . ." Shifting to a comparison between Lee and officers who had failed in other theaters, Edmondston remarked: "God grant that he may long be spared to us. He nullifies Bragg, Ransom, & a host of other incapables." The Charleston *Daily Courier* implicitly contrasted Lee with Confederate generals in the West when it noted that "Grant is now opposed to a General who stands in the foremost rank of Captains, and his army is confronted with men accustomed to victory . . . ." More explicit was a Georgian who after the fall of Atlanta gazed longingly at the commander in Virginia: "Oh, for a General Lee at the head of every *corps d'armee!*"[22]

Well before the close of the war, Lee's position in the Confederacy approximated that held by Washington during the American Revolution. "He should certainly have entire control of all military operations through-out the Confederate States," affirmed one of his artillerists in mid-1864. "In fact I should like to see him as King or Dictator. He is one of the few great men who ever lived, who could be trusted." General Henry A. Wise told Lee on April 6, 1865, that there "has been no country, general, for a year or more. You are the country to these men. They have fought for you." A letter written by a Georgian in Virginia shortly after Gettysburg lends powerful support to Wise's statements: "It looks like it does not do any good to whip them here in this state, and out West they are tearing everything to pieces . . . . But I am willing to fight them as long as General Lee says fight." A perceptive foreign observer picked up on this attitude when he described Lee in March 1865 as the "idol of his soldiers & the Hope of His Country" and spoke of "the prestige which surrounds his person & the almost fanatical belief in his judgement & capacity wh[ich] is the one idea of an entire people." Many Confederates tied Lee directly to the sainted Washington, as when Eliza Frances Andrews of Georgia called him "that star of light before which even Washington's glory pales."[23]

In line with such sentiment, Lee's surrender understandably signaled the end of the war to most Confederates (as it did to most northerners). President Davis might speak bravely of the war's simply moving into a new phase after Appomattox, but Catherine Edmondston and Eliza Andrews voiced a far more common sentiment. "How can I write it?" asked Edmondston. "How find words to tell what has befallen us? *Gen Lee has surrendered!* . . . We stand appalled at our disaster! . . . [That] *Lee,* Lee upon whom hung the hopes of the whole country, should be a prisoner seems almost too dreadful to be realized!" The first report of Lee's capitulation reached Andrews on April 18, 1865: "No one seems to doubt it," she wrote sadly, "and everybody feels ready to give up hope. 'It is useless to struggle longer,' seems to be the common cry, and the poor wounded men go hobbling about the streets with despair on their faces."[24]

The foregoing testimony indicates a widespread tendency *during the war* to concentrate attention on Lee and Virginia. Lee himself discerned the centrality of his military operations to Confederate morale (after Gettysburg he commented on the "unreasonable expectations of the public" concerning the Army of Northern Virginia),[25] as well as to perceptions in the North and Europe. A man of far more than ordinary intelligence, he read northern and southern newspapers assiduously, corresponded widely, and discussed the political and civilian dimensions of the conflict with a broad range of persons. He appreciated the incalculable industrial and emotional value of Richmond as well as the profound concern for Washington among northern leaders. He knew the records and personalities of officers who led Confederate armies in the West. He watched the dreary procession of defeats from Fort Donelson and Pea Ridge through Shiloh, Perryville, Stones River, Vicksburg, and Chattanooga. Robustly aware of his own ability and the superior quality of his army, he faced successive opponents with high expectations of success. A combination of these factors likely persuaded him that victories in Virginia were both more probable and calculated to yield larger results than whatever might transpire in the West.

Within this context, it followed that the Confederacy should augment his army to the greatest degree possible. Lee's official restraint prevented his questioning overtly the competence of fellow army commanders; however, in opposing the transfer of George E. Pickett's division to the West in May 1863 he mentioned the "uncertainty of its application" under John C. Pemberton.[26] That guarded phrase came from the pen of a man who quite simply believed he was the best the Confederacy had and thus should be given adequate resources to do his job. Braxton Bragg's sheer waste of two divisions under James Longstreet in the fall of 1863 demonstrated the soundness of Lee's reluctance to reinforce western armies at the expense of the Army of Northern Virginia. As Richard M. McMurry has suggested, the "Rebels' dilemma was that they did not have either the leadership or the manpower and matériel" to hang on to both Virginia and the West. That being the case, perhaps they should have sent available resources to Virginia: "Such a strategy would have employed their best army under their best general at the point where conditions were most favorable to them . . . . If the Confederates could not have won their independence under such circumstances, they could not have won it anywhere under any possible conditions."[27] To put it another way, the Confederacy could lose the war in either the West or the East, but it could win the war only in the East.

What about Lee's supposed over-reliance on the offensive? His periodic use of highly questionable and costly assaults is beyond debate. Natural audacity overcame the dictates of reason when he ordered frontal attacks at Malvern Hill, on the third day at Gettysburg, and elsewhere, and when he elected to give battle north of the Potomac after September 15, 1862. But these unfortunate decisions should not unduly influence interpretations of his larger military record. After all, Grant and Sherman also resorted to unimaginative direct attacks at various times in their careers. Many critics fail to give Lee credit for what he accomplished through aggressive generalship. At the Seven Days he blunted a Federal offensive that seemed destined to pin defending Confederates in Richmond; his counterpunch in the campaign of Second Manassas pushed the eastern military frontier back to the Potomac and confronted Lincoln with a major crisis at home and abroad. The tactical masterpiece at Chancellorsville, coming as it did on the heels of a defensive win at Fredericksburg, again sent tremors through the North. Lee failed to follow up either pair of victories with a third win at Antietam or Gettysburg; however, in September 1862 and June 1863 it was not at all clear that the Army of Northern Virginia would suffer defeat in Maryland and Pennsylvania. A victory in either circumstance might have altered the course of the conflict.

Too many critics of Lee's offensive movements neglect to place them within the context of what the Confederate people would tolerate. It is easy from a late-twentieth-century perspective to study maps, point to the defensive power of the rifled musket, speculate about the potential of wide-scale guerrilla warfare, and reach a conclusion that Lee's aggressive strategic and tactical decisions shortened the life of the Confederacy. From the opening of the war, however, southern civilians, newspaper editors, and political leaders clamored for decisive action on the battlefield and berated generals who shunned confrontations with the Federals. As early as the winter of 1861–62, the Richmond *Dispatch* described a "public mind . . . restless, and anxious to be relieved by some decisive action that shall have a positive influence in the progress of the war . . . ." Eight months later the Macon (Georgia) *Journal & Messenger* greeted news of Lee's raid into Maryland in typically bellicose fashion: "Having in this war exercised Christian forbearance to its utmost extent, by acting on the defensive, it will now be gratifying to all to see . . . the war carried upon the soil of those barbarians who have so long been robbing and murdering our quiet and unoffending citizens."[28] Confederate writings, both public and private, bristle with innumerable sentiments of this type.

Although Confederates often linked Lee and George Washington, they really craved a type of generalship different from that of their Revolutionary hero. Joseph E. Johnston retreated often, fought only when absolutely necessary, and otherwise fit Washington's military mold quite closely. Such behavior created an impression in the Confederacy that he gave up too much territory far too easily. A young lieutenant in Savannah complained to his father on May 12, 1862, about the Peninsula campaign: "General Joseph Johnston, from whom we were led to expect so much, has done little else than *evacuate,* until the very mention of the word sickens one *usque ad nauseam.*" Twelve days later Virginia planter William Bulware excoriated Johnston in a conversation with Edmund Ruffin. The general had avoided battle for days and given up twenty miles of ground, facts that demonstrated his "incompetency & mismanagement." Bulware predicted that Johnston would continue to withdraw, causing the "surrender of Richmond, & evacuation of all lower Virginia." Criticism intensified during Johnston's retreat toward Atlanta in 1864. "I don't think he will suit the emergency," complained Josiah Gorgas long before Johnston reached Atlanta. "He is falling back just as fast as his legs can carry him. . . . Where he will stop Heaven only knows."[29] Long since disenchanted with Johnston's tendency to retreat (together with many other facets of his behavior), Jefferson Davis finally replaced him with John Bell Hood, an officer who understood southern expectations and immediately went on the offensive.

Lee's style of generalship suited the temperament of his

people. Known as "Granny Lee" or the "King of Spades" early in the war when he seemed more devoted to fortifications than smiting the enemy, he shed that reputation rapidly in the aftermath of the Seven Days. His admittedly bloody battles in 1862–63 created an aura of invincibility that offset gloomy events in the West; that aura clung to him and his army through the defensive struggles of 1864–65. Lee's initial eighteen months as commander of the Army of Northern Virginia had built credibility on which he drew for the rest of the war to sustain civilian morale. Confidence in his army as it lay pinned in the trenches at Petersburg during the summer of 1864 remained high, while northerners experienced their darkest period of doubt. Far from hastening the demise of the Confederacy, Lee's generalship provided hope that probably carried the South beyond the point at which its citizens otherwise would have abandoned their quest for nationhood.

Nor was Lee's generalship hopelessly "old fashioned." He differed in many respects from Grant and Sherman—most notably in his rejection of war against civilians—but had come to terms with many facets of a modern struggle between societies. He predicted from the beginning a long war that would demand tremendous sacrifice in the Confederacy. He called for a national draft, the concentration of manpower in the principal southern field armies, the subordination of state interests to the goal of national independence, and, toward the end, the arming of blacks. Contrary to what critics such as John Keegan say, Lee was not a man of "limited imagination" whose "essentially conventional outlook" helped undo the Confederacy.[30] He formulated a national strategy predicated on the probability of success in Virginia and the value of battlefield victories. The ultimate failure of his strategy neither proves that it was wrongheaded nor diminishes Lee's pivotal part in keeping Confederate resistance alive through four brutally destructive years. That continued resistance held the key to potential victory—southern armies almost certainly lacked the capacity to defeat decisively their northern counterparts, but a protracted conflict marked by periodic Confederate successes on the battlefield more than once threatened to destroy the North's will to continue the war.

In late June 1863, while the Army of Northern Virginia tramped across southern Pennsylvania and the defenders at Vicksburg held fast, a letter in a Georgia newspaper described the spirit behind the lines. "In breathless but hopeful anxiety, the public are awaiting the result of Lee's movements at the North and Johnston's at the South," stated the author. "Upon their success hang momentous interests—no less to our mind than an early peace or the continuance of the war for an indefinite period."[31] This individual left no doubt about the connection between generalship and affairs on the home front. Modern students who neglect this connection do so at their peril. Any explanation of the war's outcome that slights military events cannot possibly convey the intricacies of the subject. More than that, the generalships of Grant, Lee, and Sherman demand special attention, because to a significant extent those three officers determined not only which side would win but also how long the contest would last.

4

The Perseverance of the Soldiers

Reid Mitchell

I believe if there is anybody in the world that fulfills the Apostle's injunction, "beareth all things," and "endureth all things," it is the soldier.

WILBUR FISK[1]

WHY DID THE Union win its war against the Confederate Rebellion? I find myself giving the same answer that Richard Current gave in his essay for *Why the North Won*—that, "As usual, God was on the side of the heaviest battalions." What I would like to suggest, however, is that having the heaviest battalions does not proceed automatically from having the greater population, wealth, or resources. I'd also like to suggest that the battalion—or the company and the regiment—might be the right unit of analysis to answer the question of Union victory. The ideology and the morale of the Union soldier made a key contribution to Union victory; one reason the Union could triumph was the perseverance of its soldiers.*

---

*Throughout this essay I have consciously avoided the habitual use of "the South" and "southern" as synonyms for "the Confederacy"

I do not want to go so far as to say that Union superiority made Union victory inevitable, but I will say it made it probable. James McPherson is right to point us toward a consideration of the element of contingency—things could have gone differently, on the battlefield and elsewhere, and those differences could have produced a Confederate victory. But it is no assertion of inevitability to argue that the odds were more than a little in favor of the Union.

The Union's heavier battalions are usually figured in material terms. The loyal states had a population advantage of five to two over the Confederacy—and that is counting slaves as part of the Confederate population, which is questionable mathematics. The value of real and personal property in the states remaining in the Union was three times that in the Confederate states. More important, the value of Union manufactures—as the two sides prepared to fight one of the first industrial wars—was more than ten times greater than those of the Confederacy. And the list can go on—comparative banking facilities, the railroad network, value of food crops, and so on.

These material bases are by themselves insufficient explanations for Union victory. We have learned all too well in the second half of the twentieth century that being a powerful and

---

and "Confederate." Not all Southerners were Confederate; indeed, with roughly 10 percent of southern whites Unionist and virtually the entire black population in favor of Union victory, it seems reasonable to conclude that almost half the South welcomed Confederate defeat.

wealthy industrial nation does not ensure victory against a weaker agrarian nation. The Confederacy had many advantages—a vast terrain, the capacity to put a higher percent of its white population in arms, the opportunity to remain on the defensive. One advantage it rejected as too dangerous, however, was the opportunity of fighting a guerrilla war—the one kind of warfare most likely to defeat the Union army. Once the Confederacy decided on conventional warfare, the heaviest battalions would win—as long as the Union was willing to prosecute the war.

This is the point where we are all too likely to rush ahead into good old-fashioned military history—battles and leaders—or into a study of the Union as an industrial giant and claims that the Civil War was the first modern war, or into an analysis of the social history of the South between 1861 and 1865. Let me slow us down to consider the sometimes neglected step of mobilization, because the formation and cohesion of armies—getting those heaviest battalions into the field and keeping them there—were crucial to Union victory. We must avoid treating the northern will to fight, in 1861 or in 1864, as foreordained.

A question asked during the Vietnam era may be helpful here: What if they gave a war and nobody came? What would have happened if the people of the Union had not supported the war? Specifically: What would have happened if the men of the North had not volunteered in droves in 1861? The answer is that despite the material superiority that the Union possessed there would have been no war at all—Confederate independence would have been a fact. In 1861, the Union government, frantic to establish its supremacy over the states of the South, lacked much ability to coerce the states of the North.

The reasons we have trouble imagining this have to do with our status as twentieth-century Americans. One is nostalgia. We want to look back to the Civil War as something romantic. We associate draft resisters and popular discontent with the Vietnam era, not the Civil War. We do not even consider that the people of 1861 could have decided not to support the war. Another reason we assume that the citizens of the Union would contribute the manpower required of them is because we fail to comprehend just how severe these demands were. Forever after the Civil War when the Federal government has made war, it has been more cautious about asking for so many men in proportion to the population—one reason for the so-called hundred division gamble in World War II. (The U.S. Army wanted more men but the government judged that political realities would permit no more than 100 divisions to be called to service.) A third reason is our familiarity with a powerful national state. The Federal government routinely requires us to do lots of things and most of us grumble and acquiesce. It is hard for us to imagine that the people of 1861 might have refused to serve in the mass armies of the Civil War. Yet the Union government of April 1861 was hardly the United States government of December 1941. The states, not the Federal government, created those mass armies; and for the first half of the war, men entered the armies voluntarily.

The way in which localities and states raised the troops is sometimes treated as an unfortunate concession to localism. In the absence of both a Federal apparatus for raising large numbers of men and any national tradition for such a procedure, the Federal government probably could not have mobilized the armies directly. Statewide mobilization was hardly a concession to localism; it was a necessity. The Federal government was dependent on the states. Many Americans had dealt with no other United States official than the local postmaster.[2]

When Lincoln issued his first call for troops in April 1861 he acted not from the constitutional right to raise armies—a right limited to Congress in any case—but from a statute that permitted him to order out the various state militias. While the Federal government seemed to dither in indecision, the state governors enlisted more soldiers than the War Department knew what to do with. Arguably, what saved Washington, D.C., itself, in its isolation in the first weeks of the war, was not any energy or decision on the part of the Federal government, but the speed and vigor with which Massachusetts governor John Andrew raised and organized troops, the characteristic decisiveness and uncharacteristic military competence of Massachusetts militia general Benjamin F. Butler, and the initiative and hustle of the northern volunteer soldier.[3]

Why did these men of 1861 rush into the armies? Why were they so eager that the War Department could not keep up with the enlistments and that various northern states complained that other states were being allowed to contribute more soldiers than they were? There are many reasons that men enlisted—youthful high spirits, community pressure, the overpowering enthusiasm. But the volunteers of 1861, who continued to compose the bulk of the Union army throughout the war, were motivated by ideology as well.

Their principal incentive was their love for the Union. To

them, the Union meant both the ideals of liberty and democracy that they believed unique to the United States, and the government that would uphold those ideals. They agreed with Abraham Lincoln that secession, by threatening to tear down the only existing government based on these ideals, threatened to destroy the ideals themselves. They also felt that the Union was a precious legacy, handed down to them by the Revolutionary fathers. Defending it was in many ways a familial duty, something a son owed the generations before him. In February 1862, Private Wilbur Fisk testified to the emotional strength of the ideology of Union. On night-time picket duty in northern Virginia, the soldiers marveled at their position. "When we reflect that we are standing on the outer verge of all that is left of the American Union, and nothing but darkness and Rebellion is beyond, and that we are actually guarding our own homes and firesides from treason's usurpations, we feel a thrill of pride that we are permitted to bear a part in maintaining our beloved Government." The Union was a man's family writ large.[4]

Furthermore, some soldiers of 1861 were not only pro-Union but anti-slavery as well. Perhaps only 10 percent of the Union army, they nonetheless contributed additional fervor to the Union cause. As the war continued, anti-slavery grew among the soldiers. When Lincoln issued the Emancipation Proclamation at the start of 1863, it did dishearten some soldiers, who began complaining that the war for the Union had become a war for blacks. But in general, the army was heartened by the Emancipation Proclamation, seeing it as a sign that the government—recognizing that secession was based on slavery—was willing to take the necessary means to win the war and destroy both secession and slavery. The Emancipation Proclamation invigorated the war effort.

Beyond its impact on white volunteers, emancipation was an ideological source of strength in other ways. The Emancipation Proclamation destroyed the possibility of European intervention in the Civil War. It established that what had looked to some liberals like a war for self-determination against a central government was actually a war of slavery against freedom. The Confederacy's ideology of slavery did it no good in the international arena. Just as important, emancipation opened the door for black enlistment within the Union army. The significance of black soldiers is sometimes underestimated, partly because their presence in the army is only just entering the realm of national myth and partly because they made up less than 10 percent of the army all told. In fact, however, in the concluding months of the war, black troops were more than 10 percent of the army still in the field. The union won its victory with the aid of black soldiers. Emancipation was a crucial first step in both the decision to recruit blacks and in the black decision to support a war for a Union that historically had not done much for them.

But that was a little later in the war. In 1861 and 1862 the men of the Union army were white and they were volunteers. In a war where men enlisted for a confusing multiplicity of terms—three-month enlistments, nine-month enlistments, one-, two-, and three-year enlistments—getting men into the army did not guarantee keeping them in the army for the duration. That was a problem that would particularly concern the Lincoln administration during the winter of 1863–64. Another question was more immediate in 1861–62: "How would the Union use its power to defeat the Confederacy?" That question proved difficult for the Union to answer and out-and-out impossible for many of the leading commanders, most notably George McClellan. The innovations in military technology that marked the Civil War were not matched by comparable innovations in tactical thinking. Applying the superior force that the Union possessed seemed impossible for Union generals.

George McClellan at least had strategic brilliance on his side. His Peninsula campaign certainly should have worked; the demonstrable fact that George McClellan was gutless served to discredit his plan. As a result of Seven Pines and the Seven Days, the Confederate army defending Richmond lost more than 26,000 men—nearly 30 percent of its available forces. The Army of the Potomac lost slightly more than 20,000, only about 20 percent of its forces. The strategy of taking up a position where the Confederates had to launch frontal assaults was justified—or would have been if McClellan had not panicked and retreated.

After McClellan, Union generals in the East favored "the direct approach"—march overland to Richmond seeking a decisive battle that would destroy Lee's army. But if McClellan showed that brains were not enough, Hooker and Burnside showed that guts were not either—or at least not the kind of moral courage that could commit troops to one battle in the hopes that one battle was all it took to win the war. These generals were unable to see what to do after a defeat—which makes one wonder if they would have known what to do after a victory. Thus Pope is defeated at Second Bull Run, McClellan is immobilized by victory at Antietam, Burnside and Hooker are immobilized by their defeats at Fredericksburg, and Chancellorsville, and Meade has little idea what to do with his victory at Gettysburg. In fact, the Union fundamentally decided to have its principal army, the Army of the Potomac, act as a shield against Lee's army, while its armies in the West won campaigns and conquered territory.

Until Grant came east. Grant recognized the material basis of Union superiority, and planned to bring "the heaviest battalions" into play methodically. His was a strategy not of battles or campaigns, but of war. Russell Weigley said of Grant: "He developed a highly uncommon ability to rise above the fortunes of a single battle and to master the flow of a long series of events, almost to the point of making any outcome of a single battle, victory, draw, or even defeat, serve his eventual purpose equally well."[5]

Grant believed in hitting the principal Confederate armies with concentrated forces. Because of the Union's material base, he could do this. He also believed that the way to apply this superior force was to fight every day in every theater of the war. Under his direction in 1864, all Union armies began an advance, eliminating the Confederacy's earlier advantage of using interior lines to shift troops around to where the threat was greatest. As Lincoln told him and he told his commanders, "Those not skinning can hold a leg."[6] This was a war of annihilation based on the recognition that to beat the Confederacy, its armies must be destroyed. Grant's army then was the point of the spear, and leaning behind it was the weight of superior northern population, industrial base, agricultural production, wealth.

It worked, but the human cost was immense. In fact, the human cost was so great that it threatened to undermine the military strategy, because it threatened to sicken the Union to the point it would have been unwilling to continue the war. Yankee Private Wilbur Fisk had his tongue carefully placed in his cheek when he said, "The more we get used to being killed, the better we like it."[7] Let's consider the casualties that earned Grant his reputation as butcher. During the first month of the 1864 campaign, as the Army of the Potomac ground its way from the Rapidan through the Wilderness to the nightmare of Cold Harbor, it suffered approximately 55,000 casualties—about the total strength of the Army of Northern Virginia at the start of the campaign. In the process, it inflicted 32,000 casualties—a ratio of roughly 5 to 3, which is higher than the 5 to 2 superiority that the Union possessed over the Confederacy, and is not an unreasonable proportion considering the advantages that the defense had in Civil War battles.[8]

Still, it is a little glib, even cold-blooded, to say that these are reasonable casualties. They are certainly higher in proportion to the population than the United States would accept today. So we must remember the material and ideological bases of Union superiority. First, as high as this proportion was, it was lower than what the Confederacy suffered. Second, the northern people believed that saving the Union was worth it, certainly more than the American people thought victory in Vietnam was worth its casualties, and more than Confederates thought that independent nationhood was worth the casualties Grant's armies were inflicting. Nonetheless, it was a near thing. If Sherman had not captured Atlanta on the eve of the 1864 presidential election, it is possible that Lincoln and the pro-war party would have been defeated.

The soldiers' ideology continued to motivate them through the hellish second half of the war. Furthermore, by the middle of the war, many soldiers had developed even stronger loyalties to keep them in the army. These were loyalties to their fellow soldiers, specifically to the men they served with in their messes, companies, and regiments. The jargon that military thinkers use for this kind of loyalty is small-unit cohesion. All armies at all times count on it. Added to the ideology of 1861, the small-unit cohesion of 1864 created the tenacity that kept soldiers in the army so that the Union could keep an army in the field.

Perhaps the best way to understand small-unit cohesion is think of the company as a substitute family. That, at least, is how the soldiers themselves came to feel about it. The months of service that turned volunteers into veterans also created in them dependence on their fellow veterans, indeed even a love—any other word would be inadequate—for their fellow soldiers. Leaving the army meant leaving behind men with whom one had served, suffered, and risked one's life. The affections of this substitute family competed with the claims of the family a soldier had left at home.

The loyalty the soldiers displayed extended beyond that owed to the living. As befitted "a nation founded in blood," soldiers felt bound to the dead as well—to, in Lincoln's phrase in the First Inaugural, "every patriot grave." Specifically, they felt obliged to those men who had served by their sides and were now gone, having died in the hospital or battlefield or having been sent home wounded, some of them maimed for life. Like their own families, or the perpetual Union they fought to preserve, their military families included the living and the dead. Abandoning the war meant making a mockery of their sacrifices.[9]

In the winter of 1863–64, the Union government made every appeal—and used every bribe—it could think of to persuade soldiers already in the army to re-enlist. These were the best soldiers the Union had, impossible to replace and just as impossible to keep against their wills. Without them there would be no spring campaign in 1864. There was none of the naïve enthusiasm of 1861 to call on; these men had lost any illusions about war. Over half of them re-enlisted.

That in itself suggested the commitment of the rank and file to the cause of the Union, but as a sign of this commitment it was surpassed by the soldiers' vote in the fall elections. This re-enlistment was crucial for army cohesion, but it took place before the bloody spring campaigns, with the heavy loss in life, the failed and sometimes senseless frontal assaults that eventually led to soldiers displaying a Cold Harbor syndrome and officers complaining that the men would not press attacks home. Still, even after the dreadful summer campaigns in Virginia, where the armies invented modern trench warfare around Petersburg, the soldiers of the Union voted overwhelmingly for Abraham Lincoln and the Republican party in the 1864 election—voted, indeed, for the continuance of the war.

How did the Union succeed in employing its heaviest battalions? The Union succeeded because the men who made up those battalions volunteered to be employed, not just in 1861 when they did not know better, but in 1864 as well.

Yet here we come to a question that should give us pause. Did not all the factors that created cohesion within the Union army operate as thoroughly in the Confederate army as well? The Confederate armies were built on volunteers. The experience of fighting together should have created the same small-unit loyalties in the Confederate army, and in fact it did create the same loyalties. Nonetheless, by the end of the war the

Confederate armies were dissolving. By the spring of 1865, lack of men wrecked the Confederate war effort.

In April 1865, Robert E. Lee attributed the defeat of the Army of Northern Virginia—which immediately led to the surrender of all Confederate armies—to its "moral condition." "The operations which occurred while the troops were in the entrenchments in front of Richmond and Petersburg were not marked by the boldness and decision which formerly characterized them." What caused this moral condition was "the state of feeling in the country," and particularly, "the communications received by the men from their homes, urging their return and the abandonment of the field." "From what I have seen and learned, I believe an army cannot be organized or supported in Virginia, and as far as I know the condition of affairs, the country east of the Mississippi is morally and physically unable to maintain the contest." And a less well-known soldier, Charles Fenton James, wrote his sister in February 1865 about how soldiers, listening to "the voice of despondency," started to desert. "The only fear that I ever felt was that the spirit of the people and the army might flag."[10]

It would be comforting to believe that it comes down entirely to a question of ideology—that the Confederate soldier, motivated by an ideology of freedom that was really an ideology of slavery, lacked the inner resources needed to fight the war to a successful conclusion. Or, as is sometimes asserted, that Confederate soldiers forced in the army or duped into the army, had no significant ideological motivation at all. The superior cohesion of the Union army could then be attributed to the superior morality of Union ideology.

A moment's reflection will show us, however, that this line of thought will lead to justifying the old adage that historians are camp followers of successful armies. The ability of an ideology to sustain sacrifice is hardly dependent on its moral correctness. People have endured much for bad causes. The Confederacy itself is a case in point.

Nonetheless, the Confederacy did suffer from ideological and structural weaknesses, and they were key to Confederate defeat. By ideological weakness, I am not referring to states' rights. While I do not share Emory Thomas's vision of the Confederacy as the first centralized, socialistic state—if the Confederacy was a socialist state, it was the first example of the failure of socialism—I do believe that the Confederacy's story reveals a considerable willingness to innovate within government and to create an unprecedented Federal authority. What I call the ideological weakness and principal structural weakness was the fact that the Confederacy was created as a means to defend racial slavery.

Let me give an example in terms of the very way the Confederacy chose—had to choose—to fight its war for independence. Confederate leaders insisted on organizing a conventional army and fighting a conventional war, rather than exploiting the Confederacy's potential for unconventional—guerrilla—war. Yet there was a nasty war within a war in Missouri, guerrilla operations under John Singleton Mosby and others in northern Virginia, and bushwhacking throughout the South behind Union lines. Many southern whites proved willing to adopt guerrilla warfare—what Michael Fellman perceptively calls "self-organized warfare." The Confederacy did not. With painful exceptions, the Union did not have to fight the Civil War as a war of what we now call "counter-insurgency." It is idle to speculate, but I doubt that the Union could have won the war if the Confederacy had decided to wage it as a guerrilla war. The Union certainly did not succeed in putting down what might be called the postwar guerrilla activity that took place during Reconstruction. But in 1861 the Confederacy did not choose to fight a guerrilla war—because, in large part, it did not seem possible to fight a guerrilla war and keep slavery intact.

Just as important, slavery meant that the Confederacy went to war with its population divided. Far more so than in any other American war, the soldier in the field could not count on the unified support of the civilians back home. What I would like to consider here is the way that the Confederacy's weakness on the home front—including the problem of racial slavery but considering other factors as well—undermined the loyalties of its soldiers in the field. Why did the soldiers go home in 1865?

Let's start with common sense. One reason that Confederate soldiers became demoralized was death—death in the camp and hospital, death on the battlefield, death in defeat, and even death in glorious victory. The surest way to demoralize a man is to kill him. And a lot of men went home in the spring of 1865 because they foresaw the inevitability of defeat and did not see any reason to wait around and be killed. You may call it demoralization or lack of southern will, but I would call it common sense. If it was demoralization, it would have infected anyone who could count.

But Yankees, we know, can count even better. If, on the one hand, Union forces inflicted higher casualties proportionately on their Confederate counterparts, Confederate forces, on the other, were inflicting numerically higher casualties on the Yankees. There was nothing particularly cheery about the death toll in the Civil War no matter which side a soldier might be on. Yet, as we have seen, the Union kept its armies together more far more successfully than did the Confederacy.

Confederate soldiers deserted for many reasons. Low rations made men fear for their health and doubt the ability of the Confederate government to survive. One North Carolina soldier considered deserting because the prospects for victory were so slim; he wrote his wife to "tell the children that I cant come to see them unless I runaway." Another soldier wrote, "I am tired of so much fiting for they is some part of the permotac army most allers afiting." He was war-weary—"I am tired of hering guns let alone fiting"—and he worried for his family, "my little boy was sick and Eliza was give out wek with the rumitiz." One of the most important reasons for Confederate desertion was the tug of home.[11]

"I want you to come home as soon as you can after you get this letter." This plaintive cry of a Confederate woman moves us well over a hundred years after she wrote it; imagine it impact on her husband. Indeed, some diehard Confederates began blaming southern women for men's desertion. "Where is the virtuous woman of the eighteenth century?" lamented Buck Long. "Oh! that she was still in our land to scorn and drive from door to door the cowardly deserter." Charles Fenton James told his sister, "Desertion takes place because desertion is encouraged, because the name 'deserter' has ceased, in a great measure, to be a reproach and disgrace." It was the women who should make it a disgrace: "The women of the Confederacy have the power, if they have the will and determination to save the country." The Reverend John Paris, who preached a sermon—and then published it—at the mass execution of twenty-two deserters, said that most of the men executed had been persuaded to desert by an "appeal from home."[12]

Did Confederate husbands love their wives more than Yankees did? Even a hot-blooded southerner like myself will not argue that. Sergeant Caleb Blanchard assured his wife, that "no man loves his wife better than I," and the letters to and from home testify to the depth of love of most Union soldiers for the families they left behind. But Confederate soldiers left their Confederate wives—and Confederate mothers, sweethearts, daughters, fathers, sons, family and friends—at higher risk than did Union soldiers. And as the war went on, the dangers that the people back home faced grew more widespread. Confederate soldiers found themselves torn between two duties: one to the Confederacy, one to their families. After 1864 some Confederates saw the war as likely to end in defeat; others saw it as unlikely to end at all. Not surprisingly, more of them chose their duty to their families over their duty to the Confederacy, even over their duty to their fellow soldiers.

To a large degree, the dangers that called the soldiers home came from the fact of war itself. Food was in all too short supply throughout the Confederacy. Inflation made Confederate money almost worthless—and the soldiers were paid so little to begin with. Clothes, when available, were expensive; medicine was unaffordable. Most of the grown men—the grown white men—were in the army and left the burden of farming and other work to women, the young, and the elderly. The people of the South faced a very real danger of malnutrition, even starvation. The toll the war took on the health of the non-combatant has never been successfully measured, but it must have been immense.

Other fears came directly from the Union army. As the Federal troops headed south, particularly as Sherman marched through Georgia, Confederates recognized the prospect that those they left at home would soon find Yankee soldiers on their streets, in their farmyards, and even inside their houses. The Union army was an army of invasion, seemingly irresistible everywhere except the territory just north of Richmond. How could a man protect his family when he was hundreds of miles away?

Sergeant Edwin H. Fay told his wife that "if you desire it my dearest one I will come home at any cost[,] for I hold that my first duty is to my family, my country is secondary." Indeed, his correspondence sometimes seemed intended to raise in her the fears that would lead her to call him back home. When Union forces began operating in the vicinity of Minden, Louisiana, his hometown, he advised her to wear a pistol at all times; if a Yankee insulted her to "blow his brains out." He wrote her the story of Yankees trapping two ladies in their parlor and then raping two slave women to death before their eyes. Sergeant Fay's wife never did instruct him to desert—perhaps to his disappointment.[13]

William L. Nugent was initially optimistic about the impact of Union occupation, assuring his wife "I judge you will not be in any danger at home." The Yankees would compel her to give up her slaves, but they would also "compel them to obey & respect you." But soon he advised her to leave her home, if the Union forces set up a contraband camp in the vicinity—"anything but being kept in close proximity to a camp of demoralized negroes."[14]

The women and children left behind faced more than hard times and the threat of Union armies. They faced the increasingly sure destruction of slavery; they lived among a people newly free. Southern institutions of racial oppression had been rationalized as a necessary means to control a savage people. Now the men who had been the force behind the laws of slave control were in the army, far from their homes.

Slavery, said Alexander H. Stephens in his most quoted line, was the cornerstone of the Confederacy. It was the institution that the Confederacy had been created to protect; in turn, some Southerners argued that it was the institution that would protect the Confederacy. The Confederacy could field such a high proportion of its white men precisely because loyal black men and women could be expected to perform the other labor necessary for the South to function, only because the slaves were contented and would not rebel.

And yet . . . and yet. The Old South had been fiercely afraid of slave rebellion, rebellion that might fall most heavily on women and children. And wartime slave management was not simply a concern but a matter of policy: the so-called "twenty nigger" law that exempted those men who owned or oversaw twenty or more slaves from the draft was designed to ensure effective plantation management. While slavery supposedly freed up white men to fight Yankees, slavery also required enough white men be left behind to see that the slaves did not free themselves.

The fact was, however, that the number of strong, active white men left behind to manage the plantation economy, govern the slaves, and protect white women was inadequate. Slave management was a burden that fell increasingly on women. The assurances of slave faithfulness and of black docility were never more needed. And they had never been harder to believe. Masters learned that slaves had never loved slavery. One soldier, for example, received a letter from his wife "stating that his Negroes were killing up his hogs, dogs, chickens, & c. and cutting up generally." Soldiers learned of incidents of violence, black against white; they feared for their families in a countryside filled with Yankees and newly freed blacks; even the calmest whites acknowledged a rising level of independence and assertiveness among blacks—they called it insubordination, ingratitude, and sauciness.[15]

These were the factors that undermined the cohesion of the Confederate army—not simply death and defeat but the fears men had that their families would be crushed as traditional southern society came crashing down around them. The men who answered their wives' calls and went home were hardly cowards, nor were the realists who saw the handwriting on the wall. I can only rejoice that their good sense took away from Jefferson Davis and Robert E. Lee the means of prosecuting an immoral war. The point must be made—had the Confederate soldiery remained in the field, the war would have continued, and almost certainly would have grown in brutality. And had that soldiery not gone home but headed to the hills to pursue guerrilla warfare, the war could have dragged on indefinitely—and the Confederate soldier would have come home to no home at all. If the Union army's cohesion made Union victory possible, lack of cohesion accounted for the timing of Confederate defeat. In December 1864, Lincoln spoke of the Confederate president Jefferson Davis, saying, "Between him and us the issue is distinct, simple, and inflexible. It is an issue which can only be tried by war, and decided by victory." Lincoln cast the prospect of victory and defeat as a matter of Union and Confederate will.

"If we yield we are beaten; if the Southern people fail him, he is beaten."

Lincoln's December 1864 message to Congress came after the Union army had taken Atlanta and after Union voters, including the rank and file of the army, had elected him to another four years in office. He used the message to boast of the vitality of the Union, seemingly stronger after four years of war. He pointed out "that we have *more* men *now* than we had when the war *began;* that we are not exhausted, nor in process of exhaustion." The Union could "maintain the contest indefinitely." In manpower and in the other materials of war, the Union still had the heaviest battalions. More important, "the public purpose to re-establish and maintain the national authority is unchanged, and, as we believe, unchangeable."[16] Without that resolution, the heaviest battalions could not have been brought into play. That resolution was the cause of Union victory and Confederate defeat in 1865.

So let's honor the resolution of the common soldiers and allow one of them to offer us our conclusion. Union private Wilbur Fisk, whose words we opened with, often spoke with the accents of Abraham Lincoln. In April 1864, as the Army of the Potomac prepared to begin the bloody Wilderness campaign, Fisk wrote home that in this Rebellion, "the people have not Rebelled against the few, but the few have Rebelled against the people." The "proud slaveholder" wished to destroy the government of the people and create a new nation built on slavery. Could the slaveholders' Rebellion succeed? Fisk asserted that "If the North will do her duty, we answer, Never! And the North *will* do her duty." The North would destroy the Confederate armies, the Confederate government, and the Confederate institution of slavery. Wilbur Fisk was sure of ultimate Union victory because he was sure of the perseverance of the Union soldier. "Never in a war before did the rank and file feel a more resolute earnestness for a just cause, and more invincible determination to succeed, than in this war; and what the rank and file are determined to do everybody knows will be done."[17]

5

Black Glory: The African-American Role in Union Victory

Joseph T. Glatthaar

DURING THE FINAL year of the war, Lt. Gen. Ulysses S. Grant employed his overwhelming superiority in manpower to defeat the Confederacy. Simply stated, Grant's plan was to mobilize every available man, apply pressure on all fronts, and stretch the Confederacy to enable forces under Maj. Gen. William Tecumseh Sherman to break up one of the two primary Confederate commands, the Army of Tennessee. Then, with all other forces maintaining the same stranglehold, Sherman's army was to devastate the Confederate military infrastructure—its railroads, its factories, its agriculture, and its labor supply—thus bringing the Confederacy to its knees.[1]

There were, however, numerous drawbacks to this strategy of 1864. Grant's scheme required that regiments remain filled, that states achieve their manpower quotas, and that commanders position the maximum number of soldiers at the front. This compelled states to raise more troops, an unpopular and even dangerous policy, particularly in the wake of draft riots the previous summer. As Federal armies launched campaigns in all theaters, losses surpassed those of earlier years. Such a strategy exacerbated existing hardships for soldiers and their families and created an entirely new class of war widows, orphans, and mourners. Finally, to work, Grant's strategy needed time, one of the few commodities in very short supply for the Lincoln administration. After nearly three years of bloody fighting, and hundreds of thousands of casualties, the last thing the northern population had was patience. The Union was war-weary.

In retrospect, it seems that Grant adopted an appropriate strategy for the situation, one that, if he and his subordinates saw through to its conclusion, was most likely to result in a Federal victory. But at the time the outcome was far from certain. The Union party, an amalgamation of Republicans and War Democrats, could claim little more than limited progress after three years of combat, and 1864 was a presidential election year. Some Unionists plotted to dump Lincoln from the head of the ticket, and for a time that spring and summer Lincoln seriously doubted he would win re-election. The highly touted offensives of Grant in the East and Sherman in the West soon bogged down. Grant locked into a siege at Petersburg, while Confederates apparently stalemated Sherman's forces outside Atlanta. Meanwhile, Union losses were staggering, some 60,000 in barely a month in Grant's campaign alone. To the northern public, a successful conclusion to the war appeared dim. Indeed, these were dark days for Lincoln and the advocates of reunion.

The president wisely stuck with Grant and his strategy,

and when Sherman cracked the tough Confederate nut called the Army of Tennessee and seized Atlanta, Lincoln's re-election was virtually assured. But suppose in the spring of 1864 his administration had to muster out of service one of its two primary commands, the Army of the Potomac or Sherman's Army of the West. How would that have effected the outcome of the war? Could Grant have even adopted this strategy without those 100,000 men? How would the campaigns of 1864–65 have transpired?

Such conjecture helps to elucidate, in just one area, the critical contributions of blacks to the defeat of the Confederacy. During those key months in the late spring and summer, when the picture for the Lincoln administration looked bleakest and the Union desperately struggled to maintain its uniformed strength, more than 100,000 blacks were serving in the Union army and thousands more were in the Federal navy. In fact, there were more blacks in Union blue than either Grant commanded outside Petersburg or Sherman directed around Atlanta. Their absence would have foiled Grant's strategy and quite possibly doomed efforts at reunion; their presence enabled Grant to embark on a course that promised the greatest hope of Federal victory.

At the outbreak of the war, leadership on neither side envisioned the varied and dramatic contributions that blacks would make to Confederate defeat. Nearly 180,000 served in the Union uniform with muskets in hand. As newfound laborers for the Federal war effort, blacks grew cotton and foodstuffs and aided in all sorts of construction and logistical endeavors, and as lost laborers for a fledgling wartime nation that so depended on its slaves for food production and other essentials, blacks caused shortages, hardships, and disillusionment among soldiers and civilians alike. Slaves who could not run away to northern lines supported the Union war effort through work sabotage, general unruliness that created insecurity among white southerners, and assistance to Federal troops who escaped from Confederate prison camps. Blacks alone did not win the war, but timely and extensive support from them contributed significantly and may have made the difference between a Union victory and stalemate or defeat. Lincoln himself admitted this in late 1864, when he wrote:

> Any different policy in regard to the colored man, deprives us of his help, and this is more than we can bear. We can not spare the hundred and forty or fifty thousand now serving us as soldiers, seamen, and laborers. This is not a question of sentiment or taste, but one of physical force which may be measured and estimated as horse-power and Steam-power are measured and estimated. Keep it and you can save the Union. Throw it away, and the Union goes with it.[2]

Free and slave, they tipped the delicate balance of power squarely in favor of the North.

Blacks were at the very heart of the Civil War. Although most southerners seceded and went to war first to preserve their "rights" and then to protect their homes, the issue of slavery was always central. Secessionists sought protection of individual and state rights from Federal interference, specifically, the right to own property (read slaves) and take that property anywhere without fear of loss or seizure; the right to retrieve stolen or runaway property anywhere; and the right to live peaceably, without attempts by outsiders to subvert the existing state of order, an order with slavery as its cornerstone. The ferocious aspersions that the Rebels cast toward "Black"

Republicans and abolitionists suggested the central role of slavery. In the minds of most Confederate soldiers, these northerners were the arch-villains, the group that provoked this wholly unnecessary crisis and shattered the greatest government in the world through its anti-slavery activities.

Even more obscure but no less essential among northerners was the role of slavery. While there was considerable disapproval of the institution, racial prejudices were widely held, and few of the early enlistees sought the destruction of the slave system. Instead, in most cases, Federals marched off to war for the restoration of the Union. It took Lincoln's keen mind, with his uncanny ability to cut to the root of problems, to recognize that the status of blacks was the core issue of the war, something which few outside the black race grasped. Lincoln realized that had northerners not found slavery morally reprehensible, and the institution incompatible with the new economic, political, and social directions of the country, war never would have happened.

Nevertheless, whites on both sides wanted to keep blacks on the periphery. The Lincoln administration resisted pleas from blacks "to allow us the poor priverlige of fighting and (if need be dieing) to suport those in office who are our own choise."[3] There were more white volunteers than the government could accept into uniform, and black military service was highly controversial, especially in the border states where Lincoln had to struggle to maintain Unionist ascendancy.

In the Confederacy, several states permitted free blacks to join the militia, but President Jefferson Davis had no intention of opening the Confederate ranks to blacks, either free or slave. The entire premise of such service was incongruous with the concept of slavery, as Georgia governor Joseph E. Brown argued: "Whenever we establish the fact that they are a military race, we destroy our whole theory that they are unfit to be free."[4]

Instead, the Confederacy employed blacks as southerners had done for two hundred years, as laborers. Slaves continued to plow the earth, hoe the fields, and harvest the crops, producing foodstuffs to feed the huge Confederate armies and the civilian population, and cotton with which to purchase the tools of war. They also dug trenches, erected fortifications, maintained railroads, mined essential minerals, manufactured war matériel, and performed sundry tasks that benefited Confederate troops. No doubt, in the early stages of the war, and to a lesser degree to the end, black labor was an important asset to the Confederacy.

Since whites refused to thrust slavery into the forefront, blacks forced the issue. It all began on a quiet May night in 1861 near Fort Monroe in Virginia. Three slaves, hired out as laborers on a Confederate fortifications project, slipped away from quarters, commandeered a canoe, and paddled into Union lines. The following morning, a Confederate officer approached the fort under a flag of truce. He came, he stated, to claim the runaways based on the fugitive slave law. The Federal commander Brig. Gen. Benjamin Butler refused to hand over the slaves. A shrewd courtroom lawyer and prominent politician before the war, Butler insisted that since Virginia had seceded from the Union, the fugitive slave law was inapplicable. Furthermore, since the Confederates had used these men for strictly military purposes, they were contraband of war and therefore subject to confiscation. Then, without much thought, Butler hired them for pay to construct a bakery for Federal soldiers. In one eventful day, Butler had, in effect, freed three slaves and then employed them to work for the Union army. The secretary of war promptly endorsed Butler's rationale, and two months later Congress passed the First Confiscation Act, which converted policy into law.

Together these three slaves and Benjamin Butler had struck a monstrous blow for freedom and the Federal war effort. They carved out the first path for wartime emancipation and set a precedent for military employment. Once the Federal government granted tacit freedom to runaways hired to labor for the Confederate military, it opened the door for all sorts of other cases and set the Lincoln administration on the rocky trail toward emancipation. And once the War Department began hiring blacks for wages, the practice initiated the breakdown of opposition to the use of blacks in other military capacities. First it was the construction of a bakery, then the erection of fortifications, and later labor as teamsters and cargo handlers. In each instance, blacks filled jobs traditionally performed by soldiers, which enabled military authorities to place more troops in combat commands as early as 1861.

As Federal armies penetrated deeper into the Confederacy, blacks flocked to Union lines for sanctuary from slavery. At first, Federal troops returned runaways who were not employed on Confederate military projects to their masters. This should not be, as Maj. Gen. George B. McClellan lectured Lincoln, a war to destroy slavery; rather, the object of the war was to save the Union. But for many northerners in and out of uniform, the situation was not that simple. Some soldiers abhorred the notion of returning anyone to slavery, while others found the practice of assisting masters in retrieval of slaves a nuisance that took away from their ability to wage war. It was also galling to civilians and soldiers alike that the

Federal government was aiding individuals who had cast their lot with secessionists. By early 1862 the War Department prohibited the use of Federal troops in the retrieval of runaway slaves, and four months later, Congress went even further. In the Second Confiscation Act, it freed all escaped slaves of Rebel masters upon their entering Union lines.

Precisely how many slaves found refuge with Union forces is unknown. The best estimates range between 500,000 and 700,000 during the course of the war. While some slaves traveled great distances and undertook enormous risks to reach Union sanctuary, most had to await the arrival of Lincoln's soldiers. Personal and family hardships en route, a lack of specific information on the whereabouts of Union and Confederate forces, and the real fear of capture all acted as powerful deterrents to flight. Many slaves, therefore, had no choice but to let the Union army cut the freedom trail for them.

Such was the case for slaves on the family plantations of the crusty old fire-eater Edmund Ruffin. Situated outside Richmond, the Ruffin farms were marvels of innovation and experimentation. As Federal troops pushed up the Peninsula toward Richmond in May 1862, discipline and loyalty among slaves for their masters began to erode. First a dozen fled to Union lines, while the remainder at one plantation enforced a work stoppage, despite entreaties from Ruffin's son-in-law to return to the fields. Over the next few weeks, more and more slaves slipped off to the Federals, sometimes in dribbles, other times in droves, so that by the end of June there were not enough slaves left to care for the crops and animals. Cutting losses, Ruffin's son sold much of his share of slaves and livestock and relocated his remaining bondsmen to the south near Petersburg. His father attempted to salvage what was left of his property, but the haunting question remained: Why this rash of runaways, when "no where were they better cared for, or better managed & treated, according to their condition of slavery?"[5]

With a slave population in the Confederate States of approximately three and one-half million, perhaps 15 or 20 percent reached safety with the Federals. Yet their impact was so much greater than their numbers. The war demanded a major alteration in the Confederate economy. Not only did the Confederacy have the same number of mouths to feed and bodies to clothe as before the war, but the loss of men to military service diminished the labor force significantly. In addition, the war machine consumed all sorts of material in tremendous quantities, some of which southerners had not produced before 1861. At the same time, the Federal blockade reduced the available amount of imported war necessities. The Confederacy had somehow to furnish these essentials itself, and that placed even greater demands on the laboring force. White women partially offset the manpower loss, but southerners were counting on black labor to take up the slack. Without it, workers were at a premium, commodities were scarcer, and demand significantly aided a spiraling inflation that wreaked havoc on society, driving prices up by 1865 to ninety-two times their prewar level. Thus, the Confederacy simply could not afford the loss of hundreds of thousands of black producers.

In areas such as Virginia, for example, where Federal forces campaigned frequently, the dearth of slave laborers proved critical. Soldiers on both sides, few of them well disciplined, scoured the countryside for eatables, dismantled fences for firewood, trampled fields, pilfered livestock, scattered the inhabitants, and generally wrecked agricultural output in one of the Confederacy's most productive states. Over time, Lee needed to draw more and more food and fodder for his army via railroad from the fertile Shenandoah Valley, which, remarkably, had managed to avoid the serious devastation. But the principal line, the Virginia Central Railroad, was in such serious need of repair by early 1863 that the superintendent informed Jefferson Davis its "efficiency is *most seriously impaired.*"[6] Despite a reduction of freight loads by 25 percent, the line still suffered four derailments in five days that winter due to faulty track, and this at an average rate of speed of only eight miles per hour. Repairs were impossible because laborers were unavailable. Many white workers were in the army, the superintendent complained, and black workers ran off with the Federal troops, as had nearly all the local slaves. Essentials like railroad ties, in ample supply before the war, were unobtainable, even at triple their prewar price, because there were no workers to chop down trees and make them. As a result, over the final two years of the war, Lee had to look toward the Carolinas and occasionally Georgia for more and more supplies, at greater expense to the Confederacy over railroads heavily burdened and suffering increasingly from disrepair. Nor was this problem unique to Lee's army. Overused, inadequately maintained railroads burdened other Confederate commands as well—and the southern economy as a whole.

Runaways, moreover, undercut the sense of stability in society. The thought of desperate slaves, beyond the control of whites, roaming the countryside, hiding by day and traveling at night in search of Union lines, and seeking succor from fellow blacks was deeply disturbing. It also challenged perceptions of social order. Slaves whom they had known, cared for, and looked after for years, slaves in whom they had placed trust, were now abandoning them in these perilous times in search of freedom. For Edmund Ruffin and thousands of others, steeped in the delusion of the contented slave, the situation challenged their core beliefs.

Nor were runaways the only bondsmen who aided the Union war effort. Slaves who lacked opportunity to escape nonetheless found ways of contributing to Confederate defeat. At great peril to themselves, some slaves concealed, fed, and directed runaways or escaped Federal prisoners of war on the journey to freedom. Others sabotaged farm and labor equipment or assumed an uncooperative attitude with owners and overseers, to slow down work and promote widespread insecurity among whites at home. In time such deeds paid great dividends, as Confederate troops deserted ranks to look after the welfare of loved ones at home.

Slave protests also fueled another potent weapon against southern whites, fear of servile insurrection. Revolts would have been self-destructive to blacks, particularly in the heightened military state of the Confederacy, and resulted only in brutal reprisals. But the fear of revolts brought deep worry to both military personnel and white civilians in the South. Confederate soldiers, always looking rearward, wondered whether the rumors of some massive slave rebellion this time came true. Their relatives and friends at home in turn lived uneasily, hearing similar tales and knowing they could some day become reality.

These acts—obstruction, unrest, and flight to sanctuary behind Union lines—alerted northerners to the changing conditions of the war and to the potential value of blacks toward Union victory. Through their behavior, slaves compelled Federal authorities to adapt their policies to match the increasing magnitude of the war. Originally, the objective of the war was simply to preserve the Union. Then, Federals as a war measure confiscated slaves employed on Confederate military projects, and later any slaves of Rebel masters. "So long as the rebels retain and employ their slaves in producing grains &c.[etc.]," explained General in Chief Henry W. Halleck to Grant, "they can employ all the whites in the field. Every slave withdrawn from the enemy is equivalent to a white man put *hors de combat* [out of action]."[7]

The next logical step was to remove slaves from Confederate hands and to direct their labor on behalf of the Union. Starting in 1862 federal officials placed women, children, and elderly and unfit males on abandoned plantations to cultivate cotton and other valuable commodities. The men served in all sorts of capacities with the army, from teamsters and cooks to stevedores and laborers, taking over the more disagreeable duties of soldiers and freeing up more bluecoats for combat. Whether northern whites wished it or not, the circumstances of war were moving the nation in the direction of black military service.

Among the small black population in the North, the desire to serve in Union blue was widespread. A group from Boston, expressing its commitment to the Union cause, vowed "there was not a man who would not leap for his knapsack and they would make it intolerable hot for old Virginia."[8] Leaders, such as Frederick Douglass, chided the Lincoln administration for failing to utilize its resources to the fullest: "this is no time to fight with one hand, when both are needed; that this is no time to fight only with your white hand, and allow your black hand to remain tied."[9] The war offered a rare opportunity to strike a mighty blow at slavery, dispel prejudice, and demonstrate to all that blacks could contribute in real and significant ways to the nation in times of crisis, and therefore merited full and equal rights. The best means of accomplishing those goals was through military service.

Blacks had already gained admission to the United States Navy. Perhaps as many as one in every ten or twelve men in the navy, or nearly 10,000, were black.[10] They manned ships in the blockade and fought on numerous occasions in river operations. Although none appear to have received commissions as officers, blacks served in every enlisted capacity, including gunners, with distinction. Four black sailors earned Medals of Honor, and Robert Smalls, who stole a vessel and piloted it out of Charleston harbor to safety, was a national hero.

But this was primarily a ground war, and it was in the army that blacks had to make their mark. "Once let the black man get upon his person the brass letters, U.S., let him get an eagle on his button, and a musket on his shoulder and bullets in his pocket," Douglass predicted, "and there is no power on earth which can deny that he has earned the right to citizenship in the United States."[11]

Unfortunately, in the eyes of many northern whites there was a giant gulf between blacks as military laborers and as soldiers in the United States Army. In the early stages of the war whites neither wanted black troops nor believed they had the capacity to withstand the rigors of soldiering. A Pennsylvanian who opposed black military service justified his opinion by saying, "God never intended a nigger to put white people Down," while a Connecticut infantryman insisted that black troops would be less valuable than hogs: "I think a drove of hogs would do better brought down here for we could eat them and the nigers we can't."[12]

Yet as the war dragged on from months to a year and more and initial enthusiasm waned, a transformation in the minds of many soldiers, politicians, and even some civilians occurred. "The character of the war has very much changed within the last year," noted Halleck in early 1863. "There is now no possible hope of reconciliation with the rebels. The Union party in the South is virtually destroyed. There can be no peace but that which is forced by the sword. We must conquer the rebels or be conquered by them."[13] The harsh realities of military life, the staggering and wholly unanticipated loss of life, and the lack of satisfactory success forced Unionists to recommit themselves to their cause and reexamine their approach to the war. A gradual escalation of the war followed. The Yankees learned to view the Confederate nation, its soldiers and civilians, as the enemy and were far less respectful of their needs and property. Northerners also concluded that the demands of the war, particularly in the area of manpower, outweighed certain traditional values and beliefs. It was in this atmosphere that Lincoln was able to garner support for emancipation and black enlistment outside abolitionist circles.

An opponent of slavery since his youth, the president had subordinated his personal views to the welfare of the country. But when hostilities reached such a scale and Union losses were so great that a peaceful reconciliation was no longer possible, he decided to issue the Emancipation Proclamation. Lincoln reasoned that slavery had been the major divisive issue between the North and South. A restored Union had to move beyond the slavery controversy, and the best way to do that was to place the peculiar institution on the road to extinction. Slavery, moreover, had enormous military value. Emancipation would strike a terrific blow at the Rebel war effort by depriving it of invaluable laborers.

At home and in military service, emancipation provided an ideological boost to the war effort. Understandably, opponents of slavery rejoiced. Lincoln had launched a powerful attack on America's great evil and resolved for all abolitionists a moral problem of fighting for the Union and the Constitution that protected a reprehensible institution. Despite some initial reluctance to endorse the new policy, supporters of the Union, too, recognized its worth. Even many of those who grumbled over the proclamation, especially soldiers, acquiesced in time. They could not help but notice that Lincoln demonstrated a willingness to employ any weapon to aid them in their struggle against the Confederacy.

In the international arena, the Emancipation Proclamation pulled the rug from beneath Confederate efforts to gain recognition from Great Britain and France. For some time the British and French governments had debated whether to recognize the Confederacy as an independent nation and to offer services as mediators. Although recognition and mediation would not necessarily have led to military intervention, many benefits would have accrued to the Rebels. While the French, with dreams of an overseas empire in Mexico, urged a strong, united position for mediation, the British hesitated. The Confederacy had by no means won in the summer of 1862, and large portions of British society opposed slavery under any circumstances. As Lee drove the Federals out of

Virginia and then penetrated into Maryland in August and September, the movement for recognition gained momentum in the British Parliament. But just as quickly, fortunes reversed. Lee's army fell back from Maryland after the Battle of Antietam, and Lincoln issued the Emancipation Proclamation, seizing the high moral ground for the North. By early January 1863, British antislavery forces had gained ascendancy. As Union Ambassador to Great Britain, Charles Francis Adams noted with satisfaction that "this development of sentiment is to annihilate all agitation for recognition."[14]

Still, emancipation was only part of Lincoln's policy. Its consummation was his decision to accept blacks into the army. As Douglass had explained nearly two years earlier, blacks were the largest untapped resource available to the Union. Enlistments had slowed to a trickle and Congress, hoping to avoid wholesale conscription, passed the Militia Act of July 17, 1862, that authorized the president to organize blacks and use them "for any military or naval service for which they may be found competent."[15] Lincoln, interpreting the loose phraseology to his advantage, viewed the act as congressional justification for black enlistment.

It was a bold military stroke. In one swoop he deprived the Confederacy of a great resource and converted it into one for the Federals. Not only would the Union take slaves, it would arm and train them to fight for the Confederacy's defeat.

In an unusual twist, the Federal government actually began accepting blacks into the army before Lincoln issued the Emancipation Proclamation. He decided on emancipation and black enlistment around the same time, but due to the state of military affairs, he delayed the announcement of the

Emancipation Proclamation until after the next significant Union victory, which did not occur until September. Otherwise, the Proclamation would have looked like the desperate act of a nation in defeat. With the repulse of Lee's raid into Maryland, Lincoln's pronouncement came from a position of greater strength.

Because the Lincoln administration was sensitive to the controversial nature of black enlistment, it implemented the program with caution. Less than three years earlier John Brown had attempted to seize the arsenal at Harper's Ferry, Virginia, in an effort to arm slaves, to the horror of northerners as well as southerners. To be sure, the war had altered public attitudes, and the circumstances were quite different, but racism remained powerful and opposition to the black soldier was strong. Lincoln rejected one endeavor to raise black troops on the South Carolina Sea Islands in the spring of 1862, and stalled on another in Kansas, opting to await better circumstances.

He found them in distant Louisiana, where Maj. Gen. Benjamin Butler needed manpower immediately. After the Federal occupation of New Orleans, local black militiamen had tendered their services to Butler, who respectfully declined. Several months later, however, he suddenly reversed himself and swore the men into national service, spurred on no doubt by an official suggestion he had received from Secretary of the Treasury Salmon P. Chase. The New Orleans volunteers were mostly free blacks, many of them well-to-do, with a tradition of military service dating back to the War of 1812. Strangely enough, they were militiamen who in 1861 had volunteered their services to the Confederate state government of Louisiana. Now they entered the Union army with dozens of black captains and lieutenants and even a black major.

Once the Lincoln administration broke the color barrier of the army, blacks stepped forward in large numbers. Service in the army offered to blacks the opportunity to strike a decisive blow for freedom, and recognition by whites that blacks could contribute in vital ways during this national crisis. "This was the biggest thing that ever happened in my life," asserted one former slave. "I felt like a man with a uniform on and a gun in my hand." While standing there during his first roll call, another freedman proudly recalled, "I felt freedom in my bones."[16]

In order to make black military service more palatable to northern whites, and also to serve the prejudices of policy makers, nearly all officers in black units were white. The two Louisiana regiments with their seventy-five black officers comprised approximately two-thirds of all black officers in the war. With a few exceptions in 1865, the only other black officers held posts as chaplains and surgeons. Even Butler's Louisiana officers did not last. His successor squeezed them out by 1864 under the guise of their incompetence.

The basic premise for an exclusively white officer corps was that blacks lacked the qualities to become good soldiers. Many whites believed that blacks by nature were bad material, that they did not possess the requisite character, discipline, and courage to stand up to the rigors of combat. They were lazy, irresponsible, and childlike, with a strain of latent savagery—the quality that caused southerners to fear slave revolts—none of which were well suited to the development of controlled, disciplined, effective troops. The assumption was that only the best white officers could convert them into passable soldiers.

The decision for a white officer corps proved to be a mixed blessing. Unquestionably, the policy stifled opportunities for talented blacks, and even though the whites who commanded black soldiers did so voluntarily, they were men of their time and almost always held some degree of racial prejudice. But nearly all the white officers were experienced soldiers, far superior as a whole to their counterparts in white volunteer units. They had to furnish letters of testimonial vouching for their character, and had to pass an examination on a wide range of subjects, from history to general military knowledge, and from arithmetic to tactics.

Unlike officers of white volunteers, these men knew their business from study and personal experience before they took command, and black soldiers were the true beneficiaries. Early in their service, blacks performed under the microscopic eye of northern whites, many of whom keenly hoped for the failure of this great experiment. If the Lincoln administration wanted to expand the role of blacks in military service, the first units had to perform well. Worse yet, while they were new to soldiering, their Confederate adversaries were seasoned veterans. It was especially important, then, that black troops had talented, experienced officers who could prepare them for battle.

In their initial combat experiences, black soldiers demonstrated a willingness to fight. At Port Hudson, Louisiana, two black regiments, one of them with nearly all black officers, launched several gallant rushes against an almost impregnable Confederate defense. In failure, however, they earned glory and, more importantly, respect. "The men, white or black, who will not flinch from that will flinch from nothing," penned a *New York Times* correspondent on the scene. "It is no longer possible to doubt the bravery and steadiness of the colored race, when rightly led."[17] Fortunately for the black enlistment movement, neither the northern government nor public learned that the black attackers inflicted no casualties on the Confederate defenders.

Less than two weeks later, wholly untested and virtually untrained black troops repelled a vigorous Confederate assault at Milliken's Bend on the Mississippi River, when the white Union defenders fled the scene. Although their marksmanship was poor (many had only been in uniform for a week or two), these blacks fought desperately, at times hand-to-hand, against the Rebel attackers. One black regiment had almost 45 percent of its men killed or mortally wounded, and even the Confederate commander had to concede that the black troops resisted with "considerable obstinacy."[18] The performance of blacks at Milliken's Bend and elsewhere during the Vicksburg campaign convinced Grant that emancipation, in conjunction with black enlistment, "is the heavyest blow yet given the Confederacy."[19]

In mid-July 1863, black soldiers had their most important early test, the assault on Fort Wagner. The fort protected a battery that defended a portion of Charleston harbor. That alone made it an important target, but the regiment assigned to lead the charge, the 54th Massachusetts (Colored) Infantry, aroused the attention of the northern public beyond the engagement's significance. Raised with considerable fanfare throughout the North, the 54th Massachusetts had a host of sons of important abolitionists, including its commander,

Colonel Robert Gould Shaw. At sunset, with northern journalists observing, the 54th Massachusetts stormed the works, succeeded by several waves of white regiments. None could wrest control of Fort Wagner from the Rebel defenders.

Yet in failure, black soldiers emerged victors. Witnesses acknowledged the gallantry of the 54th Massachusetts, which suffered the greatest casualties, over 40 percent of its men. Among its dead was Shaw, who became a martyr throughout the North when Confederates attempted to insult white sensibilities by burying him "with his niggers."[20] The bravery of the men in the 54th Massachusetts, and the extensive publicity they received, ensured the continuation and expansion of what the Federal government now called the United States Colored Troops.

In spite of their fine conduct on three battlefields, considerable prejudice remained. Blacks had to fight Confederates in the front and discrimination in the rear. Riding on the combat successes, the War Department accelerated its program to create black units, and at the same time meekly accepted an opinion from its chief civilian attorney, the solicitor general, that black troops should receive inferior pay to whites. Although individual black soldiers demonstrated their leadership capacity in battle, the War Department was loathe to award any of them commissions as lieutenants or captains in combat units.

High-ranking officers, too, relegated black troops to subservient roles. Many generals refused to believe that blacks could fight as well as whites and instead employed blacks in peripheral assignments, such as fatigue labor and occupation duty, where disease, rather than Confederate bullets, sapped their strength. Since some had no intention of sending their black troops into combat, they had no qualms about issuing them the worst weapons and designating very little training time. As these generals learned, however, battles occur in the most unpredictable locations, and when shooting begins, a commander wants every available soldier, black or white, on the front lines or in the designated reserve.

Of the almost 37,000 black soldiers who lost their lives, fewer than 3,000 died in combat, far below the percentage of whites killed in action.[21] That, however, represented the length of their military service and the number of major battles in which they participated and bore little relationship to their effectiveness on the battlefield. Black soldiers fought aggressively, compensating for their lack of training and experience with inspiration and dash. The knowledge that this was the "War for Freedom," as one woman termed it, provided them with an added incentive.[22] "Boys, it may be slavery or Death to some of you today," announced an officer, just before an advance. A black soldier calmly replied, "Lieutenant, I am ready to die for Liberty," and just minutes later a ball pierced his heart.[23] Like white troops, they gained confidence in themselves as soldiers through extensive service and ultimately left their mark on dozens of battlefields.

With experience and achievement in combat, too, came respect from white Union volunteers. Nothing neutralized the distrust and disdain that whites held for blacks like success on the battlefield. "I never believed in niggers before," exclaimed a surprised Irish soldier, "but by Jasus, they are hell for fighting." After black troops fought gallantly to repulse an assault by Confederate cavalryman Nathan Bedford Forrest, the Union commander admitted to a similar change of heart: "I have been one of those men, who never had much confidence in colored troops fighting, but these doubts are now all removed, for they fought as bravely as any troops in the Fort." Whether it was three hearty cheers that men in the 14th U.S. Colored Infantry received from whites for their defense of Decatur, Alabama, or the cries of "Bully for you" white cavalrymen bestowed on three black regiments after a successful assault near Petersburg, whites were admitting that black soldiers were making genuine and important contributions to the war effort. Perhaps the greatest tribute white volunteers paid to black soldiers came after that same Petersburg attack, when veterans from Hancock's Corps, arguably the best in the Army of the Potomac, congratulated the men and treated them with dignity and respect. "A few more fights like that," noted an officer of black soldiers, "and our Col*d* [Colored] boys will have established their manhood if not their Brotherhood to the satisfaction of even the most prejudiced."[24]

In a peculiar way, Confederates helped to legitimize and enhance the reputation of blacks within the Union Army. Rebels attempted to undermine the effectiveness of black units by singling them out for especially heavy fire, declining to exchange black prisoners of war, or capturing and executing black soldiers and their white officers on the spot. Such practices, however, backfired. They not only bonded black soldiers and their white officers closer, for both faced the same fate, but elevated the standing of the United States Colored Troops in the Union army. White volunteers could not help but notice that officers and men in black units incurred greater risks.

The unwillingness of Confederate officials to include black troops in prisoner exchanges also contributed in an unforeseen way. This discriminatory policy alerted Grant to the unequal nature of one-for-one exchanges. The Confederacy, with severe manpower limitations late in the war, benefited more from exchanges than the Union, and Grant halted the practice.[25]

By the end of the war, black soldiers had fought in over forty major engagements and 449 lesser firefights. Like white troops, they acquitted themselves well under good officers with satisfactory training and poorly under incompetent ones with insufficient drilling. Over all, they measured up to white troops. Lincoln himself noted in 1864: "So far as tested, it is difficult to say they are not as good soldiers as any."[26] The sixteen Medals of Honor earned by black soldiers in the war is but small testimony to their valor.

In the final year of the war, when their ranks eventually swelled above 120,000, black soldiers proved indispensable to the Union war effort. With Grant around Petersburg, thirty-three regiments were black, or approximately one in every eight soldiers. Along with the infamous Battle of the Crater,[27] the United States Colored Troops fought in many of the significant if little known battles, including Second Petersburg, First Hatcher's Run, Second Deep Bottom, Chaffin's Farm, Second Darbytown Road, Second Fair Oaks, and Third Watkins Farm.

Sherman preferred to use his black soldiers for guard and occupation duty and logistical support. Such service, while not nearly as glamorous or exciting as combat, was critical to success, especially during the Atlanta campaign, and it freed up others to serve in the front lines.

After Sherman and his army drove toward Savannah, black soldiers saw extensive action. During the Battle of Nashville in December 1864, two black brigades charged with such force that they concealed the major point of attack, the opposite flank, which resulted in a rout of Rebel forces. The next day, blacks and whites together stormed the Confederate works and contributed substantially to the decisive victory. Walking over the ground where hundreds of lifeless black and white soldiers lay mingled, an officer noticed that "the blood of the white and black man has flowed freely together for the great cause which is to give freedom, unity, manhood and peace to all men, whatever birth or complexion."[28] Several months later, blacks led the assault on Fort Blakely, near Mobile. Due to miscommunication, black troops attacked prematurely but nonetheless shattered the Confederate lines just as other Federals launched their attack.

Nearly 180,000 blacks joined the Union army, and adding the estimated 10,000 in the navy, close to 190,000 servicemen were black. They made good soldiers and sailors, on the whole no better nor worse than whites. They came in large numbers when the Union needed them most, in the final two years of the war. In addition to their military service, and their important work as laborers for the North, they helped destabilize the southern home front through their disloyalty to the Confederate cause. Thus blacks played a major role in its defeat.

Perhaps the most telling statement of black wartime contributions came from the Confederates. By early 1864, Maj. Gen. Patrick Cleburne, one of the best division commanders in the war, led a group of officers who insisted "slavery has become a military weakness." The institution turned foreign powers against the Confederacy and supplied the Union with "an army from our granaries." Its breakdown had so shaken southern whites that "the fear of their slaves is continually haunting them, and from silence and apprehension many of these soon learn to wish the war stopped on any terms." Cleburne and his subordinates called for emancipation and black enlistment in the Confederate army. They hoped that such a move would "at one blow strip the enemy of foreign sympathy and assistance," undercut the northern crusade for abolition, and expand the Rebel ranks with black troops, who would earn freedom for themselves and their families in defense of their homes. While the Davis administration quashed the proposal, southerners continued to bandy about the idea, and by early 1865 Lee publicly endorsed the enlistment of blacks. He believed they could make "efficient soldiers." He added: "I think we could at least do as well with them as the enemy, and he attaches great importance to their assistance." With Lee's support, the Confederate Congress authorized the recruitment of black soldiers in March 1865. Although this was too little, too late for the Confederacy, the legislation acknowledged the vital wartime role of black people.[29]

After the war, when black leaders tried to point out the contributions of their race to Union victory, whites began to close ranks. They claimed that blacks entered the war at the eleventh hour, and that blacks did not fight in appreciable numbers in the critical Virginia Theater until well after Gettysburg, which experts widely acknowledged as the turning point. But the arguments neglected two major considerations. Whites failed to recognize the devastating effect runaways and disruptive slaves had on the Confederacy. They also did not realize that the turning point thesis is predicated on Union success in 1864 and 1865. Whether one takes Gettysburg, Vicksburg, or even Antietam as the turning point, it becomes so only because of Union successes afterward. Those victories came, at least in part, because of blacks' efforts.

In 1861 few foresaw the pivotal position of blacks in the American balance of power. Through their actions as slaves and free men and women, blacks helped to force supporters of the Union to re-examine their approach to war. Unionists had to fight a war against the Rebels and adopt more vigorous methods of prosecution, such as the destruction of property and the use of blacks in the armed forces. For the Confederacy, they were a crucial workforce, providing food and essential labor for a wide range of civilian and military projects. Their steady loss to the Federals caused supply shortages, various hardships, and escalating inflation, all of which took a terrible toll on Confederate fighting men and civilians. Then, by converting blacks into soldiers, the Union not only deprived the Confederacy of a great resource, but employed it against the foe. As Lincoln explained to Grant in 1863, "I believe it is a resource which, if vigorously applied now, will soon close the contest. It works doubly, weakening the enemy and strengthening us." In time he proved right.[30]

The impact of blacks on the Civil War is comparable to the American experience in the First World War. To insist that blacks defeated the Confederacy, like assertions that the Americans defeated Germany, dismisses the efforts of all those others who had fought long and hard during the war. But like the doughboys in World War I, blacks helped to make the difference between victory and stalemate or defeat. They arrived in great numbers at the critical moment, and their contributions on and off the battlefield, in conjunction with those of whites, were enough to force the enemy to capitulate.

Shortly after Appomattox, Major Martin Delany told a black crowd: "Do you know that if it was not for the black men this war never would have been brought to a close with success to the Union, and the liberty of your race if it had not been for the Negro?"[31] At the time it sounded audacious, even militant; now, it sounds plausible.

Notes

Introduction

1. "Report of Col. Joshua L. Chamberlain, July 6, 1863," *The War of the Rebellion: A Compilation of the Official Records of the Union and Confederate Armies,* 127 vols., index, and atlas (Washington: GPO, 1880–1901), series 1, vol. 27, pt. 1, p. 624. I took the liberty of adding the exclamation mark after the word "bayonet." Surely it was there in 1863.

2. A. M. Judson, *History of the Eighty-Third Regiment Pennsylvania Volunteers* (Erie, Pa.: Lynn, n.d.), 68.

3. Henry J. Hunt, "The Second Day at Gettysburg" in Robert U. Johnson and Clarence C. Buel, eds., *Battles and Leaders of the Civil War,* 4 vols. (New York: Century, 1888), 3:307.

4. William Calvin Oates, *The War Between the Union and the Confederacy* (1905; reprint, Dayton: Morningside, 1974), 219.

5. Richard Allen Sauers, *The Gettysburg Campaign* (Westport, Conn.: Greenwood, 1982). A judicious discussion of the fight for Little Round Top can be found in Harry W. Pfanz, *Gettysburg: The*

Second Day (Chapel Hill: University of North Carolina Press, 1987), 201–40.

6. Raymond Aron, *Introduction to the Philosophy of History, an Essay on the Limits of Historical Objectivity,* trs. George J. Irwin (Boston: Beacon Press, 1961), 178.

7. Charles Crowe, ed., *The Age of Civil War and Reconstruction, 1830–1900. A Book of Interpretive Essays* (Homewood, Ill., Dorsey, 1966; 2nd ed., 1975). Cf. William R. Brock, ed., *The Civil War* (New York: Harper, 1969).

8. Eric Foner, "Slavery, the Civil War, and Reconstruction" in Foner, ed., *The New American History* (Philadelphia: Temple University Press, 1990), 73. Not surprisingly, an earlier volume edited also for the American Historical Association ignored the Civil War, too, both in its military and other aspects. Michael Kammen, ed., *The Past Before Us: Contemporary Historical Writing in the United States* (Ithaca: Cornell University Press, 1980). Ironically, Foner pointed out this gross distortion in no uncertain terms and with a witty double entendre: "Yes, Va., There was a Civil War," *New York Times,* September 14, 1980. See also Foner, *Politics and Ideology in the Age of the Civil War* (New York: Oxford University Press, 1980).

9. Flyer about the Avery O. Craven Award from the Organization of American Historians, 1991.

10. Roy P. Basler ed., Marion Dolores Pratt and Lloyd A. Dunlap, asst. eds., *The Collected Works of Abraham Lincoln,* 9 vols. (New Brunswick: Rutgers University Press, 1953–55), 8:332.

11. Current, "God and the Strongest Battalions," in David [Herbert] Donald, ed., *Why the North Won the Civil War* (Baton Rouge: Louisiana State University Press, 1960), 3–22.

12. Basler et al., eds., *Collected Works of Lincoln,* 8:2, 6:410.

One: American Victory, American Defeat

1. David [Herbert] Donald, ed., *Why the North Won the Civil War* (Baton Rouge: Louisiana State University Press, 1960), ix.

2. Richard N. Current, "God and the Strongest Battalions," *ibid.*, 22.

3. "Men at War: An Interview with Shelby Foote," in Geoffrey C. Ward with Ric Burns and Ken Burns, *The Civil War* (New York: Knopf, 1990), 272.

4. *The Times,* Aug. 29, 1862.

5. Johnston quoted in Current, "God and the Strongest Battalions," in Donald, ed., *Why the North Won,* 4; Pierre G. T. Beauregard, "The First Battle of Bull Run," in Robert U. Johnson and Clarence C. Buel, eds., *Battles and Leaders of the Civil War,* 4 vols. (New York: Century, 1888), 1:222.

6. Richard E. Beringer, Herman Hattaway, Archer Jones, and William N. Still, Jr., *Why the South Lost the Civil War* (Athens: University of Georgia Press, 1986), 430.

7. Frank L. Owsley, *State Rights in the Confederacy* (Chicago: University of Chicago Press, 1925), 1.

8. David Donald, "Died of Democracy," in Donald, ed., *Why the North Won,* 90.

9. Beringer et al., *Why the South Lost the Civil War,* 429.

10. James M. McPherson, *Battle Cry of Freedom: The Civil War Era* (New York: Oxford University Press, 1988), 602–5; McPherson, *Ordeal by Fire: The Civil War and Reconstruction* (2nd ed., New York: McGraw-Hill, 1992), 354–56.

11. E. Merton Coulter, *The Confederate States of America 1861–1865* (Baton Rouge: Louisiana State University Press, 1950), 566; Beringer et al., *Why the South Lost,* 64.

12. Dunbar Rowland, ed., *Jefferson Davis, Constitutionalist: His Letters, Papers, and Speeches,* 10 vols. (Jackson: Mississippi State University Press, 1923), V:84; Lamar quoted in Coulter, *Confederate States,* 57.

13. John B. Jones, *A Rebel War Clerk's Diary,* ed. Earl Schenck Miers (New York: Sagamore Press, 1958), 181; David M. Smith, ed., "The Civil War Diary of Colonel John Henry Smith," *Iowa Journal of History,* 47 (April 1949), 164.

14. Kenneth M. Stampp, *The Imperiled Union: Essays on the Background of the Civil War* (New York: Oxford University Press, 1980), 247, 251–52, 260; Beringer et al., *Why the South Lost the Civil War,* chap. 15.

15. Leon Litwack, *Been in the Storm So Long: The Aftermath of Slavery* (New York: Knopf, 1979), 189; see also James L. Roark, *Masters Without Slaves: Southern Planters in the Civil War and Reconstruction* (New York: Norton, 1977).

16. Josiah Gorgas quoted in Beringer et al., *Why the South Lost,* 351.

17. *Ibid.,* 198, 20, 333, 350.

18. *Ibid.,* 439.

19. Rhodes quoted by Donald, *Why the North Won,* x; David M. Potter, "Jefferson Davis and the Political Factors in Confederate Defeat," *ibid.,* 112.

20. Greeley to Lincoln, July 7, 1864, Abraham Lincoln Papers, Library of Congress; Weed quoted in Edward C. Kirkland, *The Peacemakers of 1864* (New York: AMS Press, 1927), 108.

21. *London Daily News,* Sept. 27, 1864.

22. Mark DeWolfe Howe, ed., *Touched with Fire: Civil War Letters and Diary of Oliver Wendell Holmes, Jr., 1861–1864* (Cambridge: Harvard University Press, 1946), 73; Medill to Elihu Washburne, Jan. 16, 1863, quoted in Bruce Catton, *Grant Moves South* (Boston: Little, Brown, 1960), 369–70.

23. Frank E. Vandiver, ed., *The Civil War Diary of General Josiah Gorgas* (University: University of Alabama Press, 1947), 55.

Two: Military Means, Political Ends: Strategy

1. Frontinus, *The Stratagems,* IV, 7.1, as cited in Frontinus, *The Stratagems and Aqueducts of Rome,* trans. Charles E. Bennett (Cambridge: Harvard University Press, 1925), 309.

2. Jefferson Davis to Kirby Smith, Nov. 19, 1863, *The War of*

the Rebellion: A Compilation of the Official Records of the Union and Confederate Armies, 127 vols., index, and atlas (Washington, GPO, 1880–1901), series 1, vol. 22, pt. 2 pp. 1071–72. Hereafter *OR.*

3. Roy P. Basler, et al., eds., *The Collected Works of Abraham Lincoln,* 9 vols. (New Brunswick: Rutgers University Press, 1953–55), 5:355–56.

4. Robert E. Lee to Thomas J. Jackson, Aug. 4, 1862, Clifford Dowdy and Louis H. Manarin, eds., *The Wartime Papers of R. E. Lee,* (Boston: Little, Brown, 1961), 245.

5. Lee to Davis, Aug. 30, 1862, *ibid.,* 265–67.

6. Stephen V. Ash, "Sharks in an Angry Sea: Civilian Resistance and Guerrilla Warfare in Occupied Middle Tennessee 1862–1865," *Tennessee Historical Quarterly,* 45 (Fall 1986), 229; Stephen V. Ash, *Middle Tennessee Society Transformed, 1860–1870: War and Peace in the Upper South* (Baton Rouge: Louisiana State University Press, 1988), 160.

7. Lee to his wife, April 19, 1863, Dowdy and Manarin, eds., *Wartime Papers of Lee,* 438.

8. Linton Stephens quoted in Larry E. Nelson, *Bullets, Ballots, and Rhetoric: Confederate Policy for the United States Presidential Contest of 1864* (University: University of Alabama Press, 1980), 99.

9. William T. Sherman to Edwin M. Stanton, Dec. 13, 1864, *OR,* series 1, vol. 44, p. 701; Sherman to Grant, Nov. 6, 1864, *ibid.,* vol. 39, pt. 3, pp. 659–60.

10. Grant to Philip H. Sheridan, Feb. 20, 1865, *ibid.,* vol. 46, pt. 2, p. 606.

Three: "Upon their Success Hang Momentous Interests": Generals

The author would like to acknowledge the kind assistance of William Alan Blair and Peter S. Carmichael, both of whom made available material he otherwise would have overlooked.

1. Drew Gilpin Faust, "Altars of Sacrifice: Confederate Women

and the Narratives of War," *Journal of American History,* 76 (March 1990), 1201, 1228.

2. Richard E. Beringer, Herman Hattaway, Archer Jones, and William N. Still, Jr., *Why the South Lost the Civil War* (Athens: University of Georgia Press, 1986), 439.

3. E. Merton Coulter, *The Confederate States of America, 1861–1865* (Baton Rouge: Louisiana State University Press, 1950), 566; Bell I. Wiley, *The Road to Appomattox* (Memphis: Memphis State College Press, 1956), chart in unnumbered section of pictures between pp. 34 and 35.

4. James M. McPherson, *Battle Cry of Freedom: The Civil War Era* (New York: Oxford University Press, 1988), 858; Josiah Gorgas, *The Civil War Diary of General Josiah Gorgas,* ed. Frank E. Vandiver (University: University of Alabama Press, 1947), 55; Benjamin Brown French, *Witness to the Young Republic: A Yankee's Journal, 1828–1870,* ed. Donald B. Cole and John J. McDonough (Hanover: University Press of New England, 1989), 400–401.

5. T. Harry Williams, "The Military Leadership of North and South," in David [Herbert] Donald, ed., *Why the North Won the Civil War* (Baton Rouge: Louisiana State University Press, 1960), 40, 44.

6. Herman Hattaway and Archer Jones, *How the North Won: A Military History of the Civil War* (Urbana: University of Illinois Press, 1983), 683.

7. Williams, "Military Leadership," in Donald, ed., *Why the North Won,* 35; Hattaway and Jones, *How the North Won,* 700, 686–87.

8. J. F. C. Fuller, *Grant and Lee: A Study in Personality and Generalship* (1933; reprint, Bloomington: Indiana University Press, 1957), 244, 242. Fuller used italics for all Confederate officers throughout his text.

9. Jubal A. Early, *The Campaigns of Gen. Robert E. Lee. An Address by Lieut. General Jubal A. Early, before Washington and Lee*

University, January 19th, 1872 (Baltimore: Murphy, 1872), 39–40, 44.

10. James Harrison Wilson, *Under the Old Flag: Recollections of Military Operations in the War for the Union, the Spanish War, the Boxer Rebellion, Etc.,* 2 vols. (New York: Appleton, 1912), 2: 17.

11. Russell F. Weigley, *The American Way of War: A History of United States Military Strategy and Policy* (New York: Macmillan, 1973), 151; W. T. Sherman to U. S. Grant, November 6, 1864, in U.S. War Department, *The War of the Rebellion: A Compilation of the Official Records of the Union and Confederate Armies,* 127 vols., index, and atlas (Washington, D.C.: GPO, 1880–1901), series 1, vol. 39, pt. 3, p. 660.

12. Beth Gilbert Crabtree and James W. Patton, eds., *"Journal of a Secesh Lady": The Diary of Catherine Ann Devereux Edmondston, 1860–1866* (Raleigh: N.C. Division of Archives and History, 1979), 648–49; Helen M. Cooper and others, eds., *Arms and the Woman: War, Gender, and Literary Presentation* (Chapel Hill: University of North Carolina Press, 1989), 73.

13. Fuller, *Grant and Lee,* 254.

14. Thomas L. Connelly, "Robert E. Lee and the Western Confederacy: A Criticism of Lee's Strategic Ability," in *Civil War History* 15 (June 1969), 130–31; Thomas L. Connelly and Archer Jones, *The Politics of Command: Factions and Ideas in Confederate Strategy* (Baton Rouge: Louisiana State University Press, 1973), 47–48.

15. Grady McWhiney and Perry D. Jamieson, *Attack and Die: Civil War Military Tactics and the Southern Heritage* (University: University of Alabama Press, 1982), xv, 19–23; Grady McWhiney, "Robert E. Lee: The Man and the Soldier, 1830–1855," in D. B. Patterson, ed., *1984 Confederate History Symposium* (Hillsboro, Tex.: Hill Junior College, 1984), 68.

16. Connelly, "Lee and the Western Confederacy," 118; Weigley, *American Way of War,* 127; J. F. C. Fuller, *The Generalship*

of Ulysses S. Grant (1929; reprint, Bloomington: Indiana University Press, 1958), 375–77; Alan T. Nolan, *Lee Considered: General Robert E. Lee and Civil War History* (Chapel Hill: University of North Carolina Press, 1991), 62–63, 71, 105–6.

17. Frank E. Vandiver, "Lee, During the War," in Patterson, *1984 Confederate History Symposium,* 23, 24–25.

18. Thomas L. Connelly's *The Marble Man: Robert E. Lee and His Image in American Society* (New York: Knopf, 1977) maintains that Lee became the most celebrated Confederate hero only after the war. Such an interpretation overlooks a mass of wartime evidence to the contrary.

19. Roy P. Basler et al., eds., *The Collected Works of Abraham Lincoln,* 9 vols. (New Brunswick: Rutgers University Press, 1953–55), 5:355–56.

20. Albert Castel, "The Historian and the General: Thomas L. Connelly versus Robert E. Lee," *Civil War History* 16 (March 1970), 62, note 50; Beverly Wilson Palmer, ed., *The Selected Letters of Charles Sumner,* 2 vols. (Boston: Northeastern University Press, 1990), 2: 268.

21. Robert Manson Myers, ed., *The Children of Pride: A True Story of Georgia and the Civil War* (New Haven: Yale University Press, 1972), 1001; John Q. Anderson, ed., *Brokenburn: The Journal of Kate Stone, 1861–1868* (Baton Rouge: Louisiana State University Press, 1955), 230, 284; Edwin C. Bearss, ed., *A Louisiana Confederate: Diary of Felix Pierre Poche* (Natchitoches: Louisiana Studies Institute of Northwestern State University of Louisiana, 1972), 126.

22. Edmondston, *Journal of a Secesh Lady,* 576–77; Charleston *Daily Courier,* May 10, 1864; Myers, *Children of Pride,* 1203.

23. William Ransom Johnson Pegram to Mary Evans (Pegram) Anderson, July 21, 1864, Pegram-Johnson-McIntosh Papers, Virginia Historical Society, Richmond, Virginia; John Sergeant Wise, *The End of an Era* (1899; reprint, New York: Thomas Yoseloff,

1965), 434; Sidney Richardson to his parents, August 13, 1863, in Mills Lane, ed., *"Dear Mother: Don't grieve about me. If I get killed, I'll only be dead.": Letters from Georgia Soldiers in the Civil War* (Savannah: Beehive Press, 1977), 258–59; Nelson D. Lankford, ed., *An Irishman in Dixie: Thomas Conolly's Diary of the Fall of the Confederacy* (Columbia: University of South Carolina Press, 1988), 52; Eliza Frances Andrews, *The War-Time Journal of a Georgia Girl 1864–1865,* ed. Spencer Birdwell King, Jr. (1908; reprint, Atlanta: Cherokee Publishing Company, 1976), 371.

24. Edmondston, *Journal of a Secesh Lady,* 694–95; Andrews, *War-Time Journal,* 154–55.

25. Clifford Dowdey and Louis H. Manarin, eds., *The Wartime Papers of R. E. Lee* (Boston: Little, Brown, 1961), 482.

26. *Ibid.*

27. Richard M. McMurry, *Two Great Rebel Armies: An Essay in Confederate Military History* (Chapel Hill: University of North Carolina Press, 1989), 155.

28. Richmond *Dispatch,* January 3, 1862; Macon (Georgia) *Journal & Messenger,* September 10, 1862.

29. Myers, *Children of Pride,* 893; William Kauffman Scarborough, ed., *The Diary of Edmund Ruffin,* 3 vols. (Baton Rouge: Louisiana State University Press, 1972–89), 2: 313; Gorgas, *Diary,* 107–8.

30. John Keegan, *The Mask of Command* (New York: Viking, 1987), 197.

31. Macon (Georgia) *Journal and Messenger,* July 1, 1863.

Four: The Perseverance Of The Soldiers

The author would like to acknowledge the kind assistance of William Alan Blair and Peter S. Carmichael, both of whom made available material he otherwise would have overlooked.

1. Wilbur Fisk, *Anti-Rebel: The Civil War Letters of Wilbur Fisk,* (Croton-on-Hudson: Rosenblatt, 1983), 19.

2. My thinking here has been influenced by Phillip Shaw Paludan, *"A People's Contest": The Union and Civil War, 1861–1865,* (New York: Harper, 1988), particularly chap. one, "Communities Go to War." He makes the point about the postmaster on page 12.

3. *Ibid.,* 15–18; James M. McPherson, *Battle Cry of Freedom: The Civil War Era,* (New York: Oxford University Press, 1988), 286.

4. Fisk, *Anti-Rebel,* 7.

5. Russell F. Weigley, *The American Way of War: A History of United States Military Strategy and Policy,* (New York: Macmillan, 1973), 139.

6. James M. McPherson, *Ordeal by Fire: The Civil War and Reconstruction,* (New York: Knopf, 1982), 411. Grant remembered Lincoln's phrase as "As we say out West, if a man can't skin he must hold a leg while somebody else does." E. B. Long, ed., *Personal Memoirs of U. S. Grant,* (New York: Da Capo, 1982), 373.

7. Fisk, *Anti-Rebel,* 87.

8. Those wishing to understand the human cost of the latter third of the war might well begin with Warren Wilkinson's splendid *Mother, May You Never See the Sights I Have Seen: The Fifty-Seventh Massachusetts Veteran Volunteers in the Army of the Potomac, 1864–1865,* (New York: Harper, 1990).

9. The phrase "founding a nation in blood" comes from Charles Royster, "Founding a Nation in Blood: Military Conflict and American Nationality," in Ronald Hoffman and Peter Albert, eds., *Arms and Independence: The Military Character of the American Revolution,* (Charlottesville: University Press of Virginia, 1984)—which is also a discussion of the First Inaugural.

10. Clifford Dowdey and Louis H. Manarin, eds., *The Wartime Papers of R. E. Lee,* (Boston: Little, Brown, 1961), 938–39; Charles Fenton James to Emma, February 7, 1865, Charles Fenton James

Papers, Southern Historical Collection, University of North Carolina.

11. John R. Marley to father, April 13, 1863, Confederate States of American Archives: Army-Miscellany: Officers and Soldiers Letters, Duke University; G. W. Philips to mother and sister, June 19, 1864, Confederate States of American Archives: Army-Miscellany: Officers and Soldiers Letters, Duke University; Neill McLeod to brother, July 19, 1863, Neill McLeod Papers, Southern Historical Collection, University of North Carolina.

12. Drew Gilpin Faust, "Altars of Sacrifice: Confederate Women and the Narratives of War," *Journal of American History,* 76 (March 1990), 1224–28; Buck Long to Sawney Webb, August 10, 1863, Webb Family Papers; Southern Historical Collection, University of North Carolina; Charles Fenton James to Emma, February 13, 1865, Charles Fenton James Papers, Southern Historical Collection, University of North Carolina: John Paris, *A Sermon Preached Before Brig-Gen. Hoke's Brigade at Kinston N.C., on the 28th of February, 1864 . . . Upon the Death of Twenty-Two Men Who Had Been Executed in the Presence of the Brigade for the Crime of Desertion* (Greensborough, N.C., 1864). Copy in John Paris Papers, Southern Historical Collection, University of North Carolina.

13. Bell Irvin Wiley, ed., *"This Infernal War:" The Confederate Letters of Sgt. Edwin H. Fay* (Austin: University of Texas Press, 1958), 96, 292, 302.

14. William M. Cash and Lucy Somerville Howarth, eds., *My Dear Nellie: The Civil War Letters of William L. Nugent to Eleanor Smith Nugent,* (Jackson: University Press of Mississippi, 1977), 117–18, 136.

15. John A. Cato to wife, March 11, 1863, The Civil War Miscellany Papers, U.S. Army Military History Institute. Bell Irvin Wiley discusses violence of blacks against whites in areas reached by Union army in *The Plain People of the Confederacy,* (1944; reprint, Gloucester, Mass.: Smith, 1971), 74–82. Clarence L. Mohr dis-

cusses rumors of insurrection, black violence, and the trouble women had as slave managers in *On the Threshold of Freedom: Masters and Slaves in Civil War Georgia,* (Athens: University of Georgia Press, 1986), 214–32.

16. Roy P. Basler et al., eds., *The Collected Works of Abraham Lincoln,* 9 vols. (New Brunswick: Rutgers University Press, 1953–55), 8:151.

17. Fisk, *Anti-Rebel,* 207.

Five: Black Glory: The African-American Role In Union Victory

1. See Grant to Sherman, 4 Apr. 1864, for the original plan. *The War of Rebellion: A Compilation of the Official Records of the Union and Confederate Armies,* 127 vols., index, and atlas (Washington: GPO, 1880–1901), series 1, vol. 39, pt. 3, pp. 245–46. Hereafter *OR.* Later, as the plan failed to work out as Grant had hoped, he adopted more of a strategy of attrition. See After Action Report of Grant, 22 July 1865. *OR* series 1, vol. 38, pt. 1, pp. 1–3. In either case, manpower was critical.

2. Roy P. Basler et al., *The Collected Works of Abraham Lincoln,* 9 vols. (New Brunswick: Rutgers University Press, 1953–55), 8:2.

3. W. T. Boyd and J. T. Alston to Simon Cameron, 15 Nov. 1861, in Ira Berlin et al., eds., *Freedom: A Documentary History of Emancipation, 1861–1867,* series II, vol. 1 (New York: Cambridge University Press, 1982), 80–81.

4. Quoted in Robert F. Durden, *The Gray and the Black: The Confederate Debate on Emancipation* (Baton Rouge: Louisiana State University, 1972), 251.

5. Betty L. Mitchell, *Edmund Ruffin: A Biography* (Bloomington: Indiana University Press, 1981), 211.

6. E. Fontaine to Jefferson Davis, March 19, 1863, 158-

F-1863. Letters Received, Secretary of War. RG 109, National Archives. Hereafter NA.

7. Halleck to Grant, March 31, 1863, *OR* series 1, vol. 24, pt. 3, pp. 156–57.

8. Morris et al., "Sentiments of the Colored People of Boston Upon the War," *Boston Journal,* April 24, 1861; "The Negro in the Military Service of the United States, 1607–1889," pp. 804–8. RG 94, NA.

9. Quoted in James M. McPherson, *The Negro's Civil War: How American Negroes Felt and Acted During the War for the Union* (New York: Pantheon Books, 1965), 162.

10. Estimates vary over the percentage of black sailors from a high of 25% by Herbert Aptheker to a low of 8% by David L. Valuska.

11. Quoted in McPherson, *The Negro's Civil War,* 161.

12. Quoted in Bell Irvin Wiley, *The Life of Billy Yank: The Common Soldier of the Union* (Indianapolis: Bobbs-Merrill, 1951), p. 120.

13. Halleck to Grant, Mar. 31, 1863, *OR* series 1, vol. 24, pt. 3, pp. 56–57.

14. Quoted in James M. McPherson, *Battle Cry of Freedom: The Civil War Era* (New York: Oxford University Press, 1988), 567.

15. The Militia Act of July 17, 1862. "The Negro," 915–16. RG 94, NA.

16. John Cimprich, *Slavery's End in Tennessee, 1861–1865* (University: University of Alabama Press, 1985), 90; Elijah P. Marrs, *Life and History of the Rev. Elijah P. Marrs* (Louisville: Bradley, 1885), 22.

17. *New York Times,* June 11, 1863.

18. Report of Brig. Gen. H. E. McCulloch, June 8, 1863, *OR* series I, vol. 24, pt. 2, p. 467.

19. Grant to Lincoln, Aug. 23, 1863, in John Y. Simon et al.,

eds., *The Papers of Ulysses S. Grant,* 18 vols. (Carbondale: Southern Illinois University Press, 1967–), 9:196.

20. Quoted in William Wells Brown, *The Negro in the American Rebellion: His Heroism and His Fidelity* (New York: Lee, 1867), 203.

21. Perhaps 80 percent of all black soldiers who died did so of disease in the Civil War.

22. Deposition of Sarah Reed, 26 May 1924, Pension File of Charles Cull, RG 15, NA.

23. Thomas J. Morgan, "Reminiscences of Service with Colored Troops in the Army of the Cumberland," *Personal Narratives, Rhode Island Soldiers and Sailors Historical Society,* 3, 19:29.

24. Quotation of Irishman in Dudley Taylor Cornish, *The Sable Arm: Negro Troops in the Union Army, 1861–1865* (New York: Longmans, 1956), 147; Report of Col. S. G. Hicks, April 6, 1864, *OR,* series 1, vol. 32, pt. 1, p. 549; Gus to Wife, June 15, 1864, Charles Augustus Hill Papers, in the possession of Richard S. Tracy and quoted in Glatthaar, *Forged in Battle,* 167.

25. Initially, the Davis administration announced that it would return to slavery black soldiers taken as prisoners and try white officers for inciting servile insurrection. When Lincoln threatened to retaliate man for man, Davis backed down.

26. Quoted in Cornish, *The Sable Arm,* 251.

27. At the Crater black troops suffered disproportionately heavy casualties and then fled in panic but with white troops "running back just ahead of them." Quoted in Cornish, *The Sable Arm,* 277.

28. General Orders, No. 5. HQ, 100th USCI. Feb. 2, 1865. "The Negro," 3512–13. RG 94, NA.

29. Quoted in Durden, *The Gray and the Black,* 56, 59, and 206.

30. Basler et al., eds., *Collected Works of Lincoln,* 6:374.

31. Quoted in Victor Ullman, *Martin R. Delany: The Beginnings of Black Nationalism* (Boston: Beacon Press, 1971), 328.

For Further Reading

A Bibliography

A fine list for further reading is provided by the works that form the underpinnings of this book. The titles that follow are organized by chapters and inevitably some titles appear more than once.

One: American Victory, American Defeat

The individual essays in David [Herbert] Donald, ed., *Why the North Won the Civil War* (Baton Rouge, 1960) and the separate parts in Richard E. Beringer, Herman Hattaway, Archer Jones, and William N. Still, Jr., *Why the South Lost the Civil War* (Athens, Ga., 1986), either advocate or challenge most of the principal interpretations for Union victory/Confederate defeat that have been propounded over the years. For a narrative history of the war that emphasizes the contingency that inhered in every campaign and battle until at least September 1864, see James M. McPherson, *Battle Cry of Freedom: The Civil War Era* (New York, 1988).

The classic statement that the Confederacy died of State Rights is Frank L. Owsley, *State Rights in the Confederacy* (Chicago, 1925). Studies that challenge this argument include Paul Escott, *After Secession: Jefferson Davis and the Failure of Confederate Nationalism* (Baton Rouge, 1978), chaps. 5 and 7; Emory M. Thomas, *The Confederacy as a Revolutionary Experience* (Englewood Cliffs, 1971), chap. 4; and David D. Scarboro, "North Carolina and the Confederacy: The Weakness of States' Rights during the Civil War," *North Carolina Historical Review,* 56 (1979), 133–49.

The theme of class conflict among whites and of the alienation of yeoman farmers from the Confederacy is argued by the following studies: Escott, *After Secession* (cited above); Bell Irvin Wiley, *The Plain People of the Confederacy* (Baton Rouge, 1943); Stephen E. Ambrose, "Yeoman Discontent in the Confederacy," *Civil War History,* 8 (1962), 259–68; Georgia Lee Tatum, *Disloyalty in the Confederacy* (Chapel Hill, 1934); Steven Hahn, *The Roots of Southern Populism: Yeoman Farmers and the Transformation of the Georgia Upcountry, 1850–1890* (New York, 1983); Philip Shaw Paludan, *Victims: A True Story of the Civil War* (Knoxville, 1981); Wayne K. Durrill, *War of Another Kind: A Southern Community in the Great Rebellion* (New York, 1990); J. William Harris, *Plain Folk and Gentry in a Slave Society: White Liberty and Black Slavery in Augusta's Hinterlands* (Middletown, Conn., 1986); and Armstead Robinson, *Bitter Fruits of Bondage: Slavery's Demise and the Collapse of the Confederacy* (forthcoming).

Several of these studies, especially Robinson's forthcoming book, also explore the impact of slave unrest and escape to freedom in weakening the Confederacy and strengthening the Union cause. In addition, on this theme, see: Charles H. Wesley, *The Collapse of the Confederacy* (Washington, 1922); Benjamin Quarles, *The Negro in the Civil War* (Boston, 1953); Bell Irvin Wiley, *Southern Negroes, 1861–1865* (New Haven, 1938); James M. McPherson, *The Negro's Civil War* (3rd ed., New York, 1991); Leon Litwack, *Been in the*

Storm So Long: The Aftermath of Slavery (New York, 1979); Clarence L. Mohr, *On the Threshold of Freedom: Masters and Slaves in Civil War Georgia* (Athens, Ga., 1986); Ira Berlin et al., eds., *The Destruction of Slavery,* Series I, Vol. I of *Freedom: A Documentary History of Emancipation, 1861–1867* (Cambridge, 1985); and Ira Berlin et al., eds., *The Black Military Experience,* Series II of the same project (Cambridge, 1982).

For a sample of the large literature on the Peace Democrats, class conflict, internal alienation, and disaffection with war policies, especially emancipation, in the North, see Wood Gray, *The Hidden Civil War: The Story of the Copperheads* (New York, 1942), which portrays the Copperheads as obstructive and disloyal; Frank L. Klement, *The Copperheads in the Middle West* (Chicago, 1960) and *Dark Lanterns: Secret Political Societies, Conspiracies, and Treason Trials in the Civil War* (Baton Rouge, 1984), which depicts the Peace Democrats as a loyal opposition; V. Jacque Voegeli, *Free But Not Equal: The Midwest and the Negro During the Civil War* (Chicago, 1967), and Forrest G. Wood, *Black Scare: The Racist Response to Emancipation and Reconstruction* (Berkeley, 1968); and four studies of class conflict and violent resistance to the draft: Adrian Cook, *The Armies of the Streets: The New York City Draft Riots of 1863* (Lexington, Ky, 1974); Iver Bernstein, *The New York City Draft Riots: Their Significance for American Society and Politics in the Age of the Civil War* (New York, 1990); Grace Palladino, *Another Civil War: Labor, Capital, and the State in the Anthracite Regions of Pennsylvania* (Urbana, 1990); and William F. Hanna, "The Boston Draft Riot," *Civil War History,* 36 (1990), 262–73. A fine synthesis of the Northern home front that demonstrates the multiple stresses and cleavages in a society at war in Phillip Shaw Paludan, *"A People's Contest": The Union and Civil War 1861–1865* (New York, 1988).

On the question of Confederate nationalism and the "lack of will" to win, see, in addition to the previously cited *Why the South Lost the Civil War;* E. Merton Coulter, *The Confederate States of*

America 1861–1865 (Baton Rouge, 1950), 566; Bell Irvin Wiley, *The Road to Appomattox* (Memphis, 1956), especially chap. 2; Drew Gilpin Faust, *The Creation of Confederate Nationalism: Ideology and Identity in the Civil War South* (Baton Rouge, 1988); and Faust, "Altars of Sacrifice: Confederate Women and the Narratives of War," *Journal of American History,* 76 (1990), 1200–1228.

The literature on strategy, logistics, and generalship is discussed below in the bibliographies for Chapters 2 and 3.

Comparisons of the leadership qualities of Jefferson Davis and Abraham Lincoln can be found in almost any biography of either man. Most of them emphasize Lincoln's superiority in this respect: see especially Colin R. Ballard, *The Military Genius of Abraham Lincoln* (London, 1926); Maurice Frederick, *Statesmen and Soldiers of the Civil War: A Study of the Conduct of War* (1926); and James M. McPherson, *Abraham Lincoln and the Second American Revolution* (New York, 1991). See also Herman Hattaway and Archer Jones, "Lincoln as a Military Strategist," *Civil War History,* 26 (1980), 293–303. On Davis, consult Frank E. Vandiver, "Jefferson Davis and Confederate Strategy," in Frank E. Vandiver and Avery Craven, eds., *The American Tragedy: The Civil War in Retrospect* (Hampden-Sydney, 1959), and Grady McWhiney, "Jefferson Davis and the Art of War," *Civil War History,* 21 (1975), 101–12.

Two: Military Means: Political Ends: Strategy

In 1956 Frank E. Vandiver provided a durable and discerning look at Confederate Strategy in his *Rebel Brass* (Baton Rouge). Presenting a comprehensive and very influential interpretation of Union strategy in his *Lincoln and His Generals* (New York, 1952), T. Harry Williams then related it to Jomini and to the Confederacy in his "The Military Leadership of North and South" in David [Herbert] Donald, ed., *Why the North Won the Civil War* (Baton Rouge,

1960). Stephen E. Ambrose used this approach in his *Halleck: Lincoln's Chief of Staff* (Baton Rouge, 1962), and Russell Weigley interpreted Lee as well as Grant as seeking decision in battle in his *American Way of War* (New York, 1973). In their *How the North Won: A Military History of the Civil War* (Urbana, 1983), Herman Hattaway and Archer Jones offered a new interpretation of Lincoln as well as of both generals and a comprehensive view of strategy; they also sought to close nearly two decades of writing on Jomini and the Civil War by arguing against his influence. Weigley then synthesized much of the foregoing in his "American Strategy from Its Beginnings to the First World War" in Peter Paret, ed., *Makers of Modern Strategy from Machiavelli to the Nuclear Age* (Princeton, 1986). In Paret's book is also a conclusive essay on Jomini by John Shy.

In his *Middle Tennessee Transformed: War and Peace in the Upper South* (Baton Rouge, 1988), Stephen V. Ash includes an excellent treatment of guerrilla warfare. Larry E. Nelson, *Bullets, Ballots, and Rhetoric: Confederate Policy for the United States Presidential Contest of 1864* (University: University of Alabama Press, 1980), sheds light on the connection between military strategy and political objectives. In his *Lifeline of the Confederacy: Blockade Running During the Civil War* (Columbia, S.C., 1988), Stephen R. Wise shows the ineffectiveness of the blockade. Edward Hagerman's *The American Civil War and the Origin of Modern War: Ideas, Organization, and Field Command* (Bloomington, 1988) makes a valuable contribution by underpinning strategy with his knowledge of tactics and logistics. Richard M. McMurry, *Two Great Rebel Armies: An Essay in Confederate Military History* (Chapel Hill, 1989), examines many interpretations of strategy as well as the armies of Tennessee and Northern Virginia. Archer Jones, *Civil War Command and Strategy* (New York, 1992), seeks to comprehend all of the foregoing and has an extensive bibliographic note.

Three: "Upon their Success Hang Momentous Interests": Generals

The literature touching on generalship during the Civil War is staggering in size and quite uneven in quality. Herman Hattaway and Archer Jones, *How the North Won: A Military History of the Civil War* (Urbana, 1983), and Russell F. Weigley, *The American Way of War* (New York, 1973), serve as excellent starting points. Two other standard works that reach conclusions quite different from those of Hattaway and Jones are T. Harry Williams's *Lincoln and His Generals* (New York, 1952), and "The Military Leadership of North and South," in David [Herbert] Donald, ed., *Why the North Won the Civil War* (Baton Rouge, 1960). On the Confederate side, Richard M. McMurry, *Two Great Rebel Armies: An Essay in Confederate Military History* (Chapel Hill, 1989) combines astute observations and a touch of humor. Thomas L. Connelly and Archer Jones, *The Politics of Command: Factions and Ideas in Confederate Strategy* (Baton Rouge, 1973) focuses on the tension between Lee and the "Western Concentration Bloc." Steven Woodworth, *Jefferson Davis and His Generals: The Failure of Confederate Command in the West* (Lawrence, 1990), demonstrates why so little good news for the South emanated from west of the Appalachian Mountains. Grady McWhiney and Perry D. Jamieson, *Attack and Die: Civil War Military Tactics and the Southern Heritage* (University, 1982), melds cultural and military history to construct a controversial interpretation of failure among Confederate generals.

A number of studies shed light on the principal commanders. J. F. C. Fuller argues for Grant's greatness in *Grant and Lee: A Study in Personality and Generalship* and *The Generalship of Ulysses S. Grant* (originally published in 1932 and 1929 respectively; reprint, Bloomington, 1957, 1958). Two perceptive, and largely favorable, interpretations of Grant may be found in John Keegan, *The Mask of Command* (New York, 1987), and T. Harry Williams, *McClellan,*

Sherman, and Grant (New Brunswick, 1962). On Grant's great lieutenant, see Charles Royster, *The Destructive War: William Tecumseh Sherman, Stonewall Jackson, and the Americans* (New York, 1991), B. H. Liddell-Hart, *Sherman: Soldier, Realist, American* (New York, 1929), and Joseph T. Glatthaar, *The March to the Sea and Beyond: Sherman's Troops in the Savannah and Carolinas Campaigns* (New York, 1985).

Any examination of Lee as a soldier must still begin with Douglas Southall Freeman's massive and admiring *R. E. Lee: A Biography,* 4 vols. (New York, 1934–36). The chapter titled "The Sword of Robert E. Lee" in vol. 4 contains the essence of Freeman's analysis. It is worth mentioning that some later critics of Lee, most notably Thomas L. Connelly, attacked Freeman as much as Lee in their critiques of the general. Other necessary studies include Connelly's starkly revisionist *The Marble Man: Robert E. Lee and His Image in American Society* (New York, 1977); Alan T. Nolan's more judicious re-examination *Lee Considered: General Robert E. Lee and Civil War History* (Chapel Hill, 1991); Charles P. Roland's favorable "The Generalship of Robert E. Lee," in Grady McWhiney, ed., *Grant, Lee, Lincoln and the Radicals* (N.p.: Northwestern University Press, 1964); and Albert Castel's response to Connelly titled "The Historian and the General: Thomas L. Connelly versus Robert E. Lee," in *Civil War History,* 16 (March 1970), 50–63.

Three other books belong on any short shelf of works relating to the subject of generalship during war. As its title implies, Edward Hagerman, *The American Civil War and the Origins of Modern Warfare* (Bloomington, 1988) believes that the conflict anticipated modern wars, a position with which Paddy Griffith's *Battle Tactics of the Civil War* (New Haven, 1987) takes sharp issue. Finally, Michael C. C. Adams, *Our Masters the Rebels: A Speculation on Union Military Failure in the East, 1861–1865* (Cambridge, Mass., 1978), suggests that a false perception of Lee's superiority hamstrung Federal commanders in the Virginia theater.

For a sampling of recent works that discuss the reasons for Confederate defeat without making connections between the military and civilian spheres, see Gary W. Gallagher, "Home Front and Battlefield: Some Recent Literature Relating to Virginia and the Confederacy," *Virginia Magazine of History and Biography* 98 (April 1990), 135–68. Older studies that emphasized loss of civilian morale without dwelling on links to military events include Bell I. Wiley, *The Plain People of the Confederacy* (Baton Rouge, 1943), Charles W. Ramsdell, *Behind the Lines in the Southern Confederacy* (Baton Rouge, 1944), and Kenneth M. Stampp, "The Southern Road to Appomattox," in *The Imperiled Union: Essays on the Background of the Civil War* (New York, 1980).

Four: The Perseverance of The Soldiers

For analyses of those aspects of the war that are traditionally considered "military" (although any military consideration of the Civil War rapidly becomes technological, political, economic, and social) and specifically of the question of why the Union won, see David [Herbert] Donald, ed., *Why the North Won the Civil War* (Baton Rouge, 1960), particularly Richard N. Current's "God and the Strongest Battalions." See also James M. McPherson, *Ordeal by Fire: The Civil War and Reconstruction* (2nd ed., New York, 1992), and *The Battle Cry of Freedom* (New York, 1988); Richard E. Beringer et al., *Why the South Lost the Civil War* (Athens, 1986); and especially Russell Weigley, *The American Way of War* (New York, 1973). While not about the Civil War, John Keegan, *The Face of Battle* (New York, 1976), is indispensable for understanding how armies work. Phillip Shaw Paludan, *"A People's Contest": The Union and the Civil War, 1861–1865* (New York, 1988), is crucial for understanding the Union war effort. See also my own piece "The Northern Soldier and His Community," In Maris Vinovskis, ed., *Towards a Social History of the American Civil War* (New York,

1990). Emory M. Thomas has presented intelligent and provocative interpretation in *The Confederate Nation 1861–1865* (New York, 1979). Michael Fellman's *Inside War* (New York, 1989) is an intriguing analysis of guerrilla warfare in Missouri. Recent work on soldiers of the Civil War includes Earl Hess, *Liberty, Virtue, and Progress* (New York, 1988), Randall Jimerson, *The Private Civil War* (Baton Rouge, 1988), Gerald Linderman, *Embattled Courage* (New York, 1987), and Reid Mitchell, *Civil War Soldiers* (New York, 1988).

Bell Irvin Wiley was a pioneer historian of the social experience of the Civil War. His work is still essential. His two volumes on soldier life, *The Life of Johnny Reb* (Indianapolis, 1943) and *The Life of Billy Yank* (Indianapolis, 1952), are his best known, but it was in his *Plain People of the Confederacy* (Baton Rouge, 1943) that he dealt most cogently with the issue of Confederate morale. See also his *Southern Negroes 1861–1865* (New Haven, 1938) and *The Road to Appomattox* (Memphis, 1956).

Five: Black Glory: The African-American Role in Union Victory

The best overview of blacks in the Union army is Dudley Taylor Cornish, *The Sable Arm: Negro Troops in the Union Army, 1861–1865* (1956; reprint, Lawrence, 1987). Influenced by the "new" military history, which seeks to study the impact of the military establishment on individuals and society, Joseph T. Glatthaar, *Forged in Battle: The Civil War Alliance of Black Soldiers and White Officers* (New York, 1990), analyzes the relationship of white officers and black soldiers and provides the reader with a sense of what service in the United States Colored Troops was like. Also worth reading are W. E. B. Du Bois, *Black Reconstruction in America* (New York, 1935), and George Washington Williams, *A History of the Negro Troops in the War of the Rebellion, 1861–1865* (1888; reprint, New

York, 1969). Williams served as an enlisted man in a black regiment.

James M. McPherson, *The Negro's Civil War: How American Negroes Felt and Acted During the War for the Union* (New York, 1965), and Ira Berlin, et al., ed., *Freedom: A Documentary History of Emancipation,* series II, vol. 1 (Cambridge, 1982), are excellent primary source collections on black soldiers in the war. Both have valuable essays as well. Still another great collection of documents, available on microfilm through the National Archives, is "The Negro in the Military Service of the United States, 1607–1889," in six reels.

There are many fine wartime memoirs of both black soldiers and white officers. Three of the best are Alexander H. Newton, *Out of the Briars: An Autobiography and Sketch of the Twenty-Ninth Regiment Connecticut Volunteers* (1910; reprint, Miami, 1969); the classic *Army Life in a Black Regiment* (1869; reprint, New York, 1984) by Thomas Wentworth Higginson; and Luis F. Emilio, *A Brave Black Regiment: History of the Fifty-Fourth Regiment of Massachusetts Volunteer Infantry* (1894; reprint, New York, 1969). An extensive bibliography of published primary sources may be found in Glatthaar, *Forged in Battle.*

Along with Cornish's work, two books that have stood the test of time are Benjamin Quarles, *The Negro in the Civil War* (1953; reprint, New York, 1989) and Bell I. Wiley, *Southern Negroes, 1861–1865* (1935; reprint, Baton Rouge, 1974). Both volumes place black military service in the larger context of the black experience during the war.

Very little is known of black naval service. The best large-scale study, David L. Valuska, "The Negro in the Union Navy, 1861–1865," a dissertation at Lehigh University in 1973, has not found its way into print yet. Herbert Aptheker's article entitled "Negro in the Union Navy" is the best published piece. This, along with other interesting essays of his, are in *To Be Free: Studies in American Negro History* (1948; reprint, New York, 1968).

In recent years, there has been a plethora of wonderful volumes detailing the transition of blacks from slavery to freedom. A few of the best are Leon Litwack, *Been in the Storm So Long: The Aftermath of Slavery* (New York, 1978), Joel Williamson, *After Slavery: The Negro in South Carolina During Reconstruction, 1861–1877* (Chapel Hill, 1965), and Barbara J. Fields, *Slavery and Freedom on the Middle Ground* (New Haven, 1985). Willie Lee Rose, *Rehearsal for Reconstruction: The Port Royal Experiment* (1964; reprint, New York, 1976), details the Port Royal experiment well. Lawrence N. Powell, *New Masters: Northern Planters During the Civil War and Reconstruction* (New Haven, 1980), and Eric Foner, *Reconstruction: America's Unfinished Revolution, 1863–1877* (New York, 1988), cover Union employment of freedmen in the South during the war. By comparison, very little exists on blacks in the North during the war.

For insights into Lincoln's decision to emancipate slaves, see LaWanda Cox, *Lincoln and Black Freedom: A Study in Presidential Leadership* (Columbia, S.C., 1981), and John Hope Franklin, *The Emancipation Proclamation* (1963; reprint, Garden City, 1965). Gabor S. Boritt's essay titled "The Voyage to the Colony of Linconia," *Historian,* 37 (August 1975), 619–32, applies the psychological concept of avoidance to Lincoln's attitudes toward black colonization beyond the borders of the United States.

On the Confederate debate over black enlistment, Robert F. Durden, *The Gray and the Black: The Confederate Debate on Emancipation* (Baton Rouge, 1972), is the place to begin. Little is known of the Confederate black troops, raised very late in the war.

The best studies on racial attitudes are David Brion Davis, *The Problem of Slavery in Western Culture* (Ithaca, 1966), Winthrop Jordan, *White Over Black: American Attitudes Toward the Negro, 1550–1812* (1969; reprint, New York, 1977), and George M. Frederickson, *The Black Image in the White Mind: The Debate on Afro-American Character and Destiny, 1817–1914* (New York, 1971).

Contributors

James M. McPherson, born in North Dakota and raised in Minnesota, holds degrees from Gustavus Adolphus College (B.A.) and Johns Hopkins University (Ph.D.). Since 1962 he has taught at Princeton University, where he serves as the George Henry Davis '86 Professor of American History. His books include *Battle Cry of Freedom: The Civil War Era* (1988), which won the Pulitzer Prize in History for 1989; *Abraham Lincoln and the Second American Revolution* (1991); and *Ordeal by Fire: The Civil War and Reconstruction,* 2nd edition (1992).

Archer Jones, born and raised in Virginia, holds degrees from Hampden-Sydney College (B.A.) and the University of Virginia (Ph.D.). He has served as Professor of History and a

Dean at North Dakota State University and as Morrison Professor at the U.S. Army Command and General Staff College. He is co-author of *How the North Won* (1983) and *Why the South Lost the Civil War* (1986), and author of *Confederate Strategy from Shiloh to Vicksburg* (1961, 1991) and *The Art of War in the Western World* (1987).

Gary W. Gallagher, born in California and raised in Colorado, holds degrees from Adams State College (B.A.) and the University of Texas at Austin (M.A., Ph.D.). He is Head of the Department of History at Pennsylvania State University. He is the author of *Stephen Dodson Ramseur: Lee's Gallant General* (1985), editor of *Fighting for the Confederacy: The Personal Recollections of General Edward Porter Alexander* (1989), and editor and co-author of *Antietam: Essays on the 1862 Maryland Campaign* (1989) and *Struggle for the Shenandoah: Essays on the 1864 Valley Campaign* (1991).

Reid Mitchell, born in Georgia and raised in Louisiana, holds degrees from the University of New Orleans (B.A.), William and Mary (M.A.), and the University of California, Berkeley (Ph.D.). He has taught at the University of New Orleans, the University of California, and Rutgers University. He is Assistant Professor of History at Princeton University and author of *Civil War Soldiers* (1988).

Joseph T. Glatthaar, born and raised in New York, holds degrees from Ohio Wesleyan University (B.A.), Rice University (M.A.), the University of Wisconsin-Madison (Ph.D.), and is the Head of the Department of History at the University of Houston. He has also taught at the University of

Wisconsin, the U.S. Army Command and General Staff College, and the U.S. Army War College. His books include *The March to the Sea and Beyond: Sherman's Troops in the Savannah and Carolinas Campaigns* (1985) and *Forged in Battle: The Civil War Alliance of Black Soldiers and White Officers* (1990).

Gabor S. Boritt, born and raised in Hungary, holds degrees from Yankton College, S.D. (B.A.), the University of South Dakota (M.A.), and Boston University (Ph.D.). He serves as the Fluhrer Professor of Civil War Studies, and Director, Civil War Institute, Gettysburg College. He has held visiting appointments at Harvard, Cambridge, and the University of Michigan, Ann Arbor. He is the author of *Lincoln and the Economics of the American Dream* (1978), co-author of *The Lincoln Image* (1984) and *The Confederate Image* (1987), and co-author and editor of *The Historian's Lincoln* (1988).

Index